CLASSICAL MECHANICS

B. P. Cowan

Lecturer in Physics
Bedford College, University of London

ROUTLEDGE & KEGAN PAUL
London, Boston, Melbourne and Henley

First published in 1984
by Routledge & Kegan Paul plc

39 Store Street, London WC1E 7DD, England
9 Park Street, Boston, Mass. 02108, USA

464 St Kilda Road, Melbourne,
Victoria 3004, Australia and

Broadway House, Newtown Road,
Henley-on-Thames, Oxon RG9 1EN, England

Set in Press Roman by Hope Services, Abingdon
and printed in Great Britain
by Cox & Wyman Ltd., Reading

Library of Congress Cataloging in Publication Data

Cowan, B. P., 1951–

Classical mechanics.
(Student physics series)
Includes index.
1. Mechanics.   I. Title.   II. Series.
QA805.C78   1984   531   83-26904

British Library CIP Data available

ISBN 0-7102-0280-6

CLASSICAL MECHANICS

Contents

Preface

The study of mechanics plays a central role in physics for a whole variety of reasons. It was one of the earliest of the quantitative sciences, and had immediate practical applications. These ranged from the study of the motion of projectiles in warfare to the motion of the planets, predicting the seasons, eclipses, etc. At the present time, even though superseded on the very small scale by quantum theory and on the very large scale by the theory of relativity, the mechanics of Newton is perfectly adequate for treating a wide spectrum of problems from the ' 'netic theory of gases to the motion of space vehicles. Furthermore, the science of mechanics is regarded by many as the epitome of a good scientific theory and for this reason is studied by philosophers and social scientists alike as an exemplar of the 'scientific method'. We shall commence in Chapter 1 with a brief historical outline of the development of mechanics, mentioning the names and dates of the main participants and summarizing their contributions.

Chapter 1
Newton's laws

1.1 Historical introduction

Primitive ideas about mechanics were exemplified by the statements of Aristotle (384-322 BC), who asserted that a force was
necessary to maintain motion. Furthermore, he believed that there
were different laws for heavenly and earthly bodies. On earth,
bodies tended to move in straight lines whereas in the heavens
bodies moved in circles, perfect figures 'having no beginning and
no end'. To maintain them in motion, Aristotle believed that
there were angels pushing the planets round in their orbits!

Mechanics then had to wait for Galileo (1564-1642) to study
these ideas both experimentally and theoretically. He came to
the conclusion that forces change the motion, that, ideally,
uniform motion in a straight line occurs in the absence of force.
On rolling a ball down an inclined plane he observed it to accelerate. As the gradient of the slope was decreased the acceleration
also decreased. Thus he concluded that on a level surface the ball
would continue at constant speed, neglecting friction.

These ideas were taken over and developed further by Newton
(1642-1727), who actually took Galileo's findings above as the
first of his famous three laws of motion. This was a special case of
Newton's second law, briefly stated, that 'the acceleration of a
body multiplied by its mass is equal to the force applied'. Together
with his third law, 'that action and reaction are equal', these laws
enabled mechanical problems to be solved once the force was
specified. We shall discuss Newton's laws in greater detail in
section 1.3.

It was realized by Mach (1839-1916) that there were logical flaws in Newton's laws when taken with his definitions of mass, length and time. He reformulated the laws of motion in a consistent operational form; in fact Einstein (1879-1955), seeing this critical analysis, was influenced in his development of the theory of relativity. However, mathematically Mach's formulation of mechanics is equivalent to Newton's (whereas Einstein's is not). Nevertheless, for simplicity and for conformity with most elementary treatments of mechanics, we shall follow the Newtonian formulation. (In section 1.5, however, we shall give a brief discussion of Mach's treatment.)

Newton made another important contribution to the science of mechanics, in his Universal Law of Gravitation, which states: two bodies attract each other with a force inversely proportional to the square of their separation. (Gravitation is discussed in section 3.7.) The development of the law of gravitation was based on astronomical observations.

Tycho Brahe (1546-1601) was a Danish astronomer who made careful observations of the planets. He believed that the earth was at the centre of the universe and that the planets moved around the earth in circles, but he did not let this influence his work. His extensive collection of data was studied by Kepler (1571-1630), who was originally appointed by Tycho Brahe as his assistant.

Kepler discovered that the great mass of data was consistent with three laws, which he enunciated as follows:

1. The path of a planet is an ellipse with the sun at one focus.
2. The line joining the planet to the sun sweeps out equal areas in equal times.
3. The square of the orbital period is proportional to the cube of the distance from the sun.

Newton took these three laws of Kepler and, using his own laws of motion, concluded that the planets were attracted to the sun in accordance with the Universal Law of Gravitation. There is a further conceptual advance here, since heavenly and earthly bodies are seen to obey the same laws of motion.

Further developments in mechanics will be discussed in chapter 6, but they are essentially nothing more than sophisticated reformulations of Newton's laws. However, it must not be thought that classical mechanics is a closed book. There are still areas of research active today. One of these is the study of the highly chaotic behaviour of complex dynamical systems. Another is the question of dynamic stability, of particular importance for the plasmas in nuclear fusion reactors. Unfortunately these are both beyond the scope of this book.

1.2 Kinematics and the use of vectors

By kinematics we mean the description of motion without enquiring as to the cause of the motion. The position of a particle in three-dimensional space is given by a vector, say **r**, called the position vector. Its motion or *trajectory* is given by specifying the position vector for all times—in other words a vector function of time, **r**(*t*).

Newton actually invented the calculus while developing his ideas on mechanics. He appreciated the importance of the 'rate of change' of various quantities, as we shall see. In this spirit we are immediately led to the idea of velocity as the rate of change of position. The velocity vector **v** is defined by:

$$\mathbf{v} = \frac{d\mathbf{r}}{dt} \tag{1.1}$$

where the differentiation of a vector function of a scalar is given by the usual limiting procedure,

$$\mathbf{v}(t) = \lim_{\epsilon \to 0} \frac{\mathbf{r}(t + \epsilon) - \mathbf{r}(t)}{\epsilon}. \tag{1.2}$$

Differentiation with respect to time is also denoted by a dot above the quantity, so that the velocity may also be written as

$$\mathbf{v}(t) = \dot{\mathbf{r}}(t). \tag{1.3}$$

The velocity vector is always tangential to the motion, which may be seen from Fig. 1.1. Furthermore, for a particle moving in a straight line the velocity is collinear with the motion.

Nature is such that the derivative of the velocity also plays an important role. The laws of mechanics are formulated in terms of

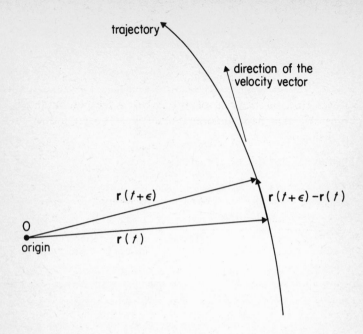

Fig. 1.1 The velocity vector is tangential to the trajectory

the position vector together with its first and second derivatives; higher derivatives are found to play no part. Thus, we also consider the acceleration **a**, the time derivative of the velocity:

$$\mathbf{a} = \frac{d\mathbf{v}}{dt} = \frac{d^2\mathbf{r}}{dt^2} \qquad [1.4]$$

or

$$\mathbf{a} = \dot{\mathbf{v}} = \ddot{\mathbf{r}}.$$

Example 1.1

What is the trajectory of a particle moving with constant velocity? (Remember that constant velocity means both constant magnitude – speed – and constant direction.)

If the velocity is constant we may integrate equation [1.1] immediately:

$$\mathbf{r}(t) = \mathbf{r}(0) + \int_0^t \mathbf{v}\,\mathrm{d}t'$$

$$= \mathbf{r}(0) + \mathbf{v}t$$

where $\mathbf{r}(0)$, the constant of integration, is the positon at zero time. We thus have uniform motion in a straight line in the direction of $\mathbf{v}$.

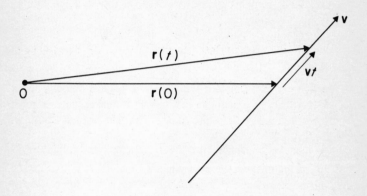

Fig. 1.2 Rectilinear motion at constant velocity

Example 1.2

Find the trajectory of a particle moving with constant acceleration $\mathbf{a}$.

If the acceleration is constant we may integrate equation [1.4] to find the velocity

$$\mathbf{v}(t) = \mathbf{v}(0) + \int_0^t \mathbf{a}\,\mathrm{d}t'$$

or

$$\mathbf{v}(t) = \mathbf{v}(0) + \mathbf{a}t.$$

This must be integrated once more to find the trajectory

$$\mathbf{r}(t) = \mathbf{r}(0) + \int_0^t \mathbf{v}(t')\,\mathrm{d}t'$$

$$= \mathbf{r}(0) + \int_0^t (\mathbf{v}(0) + \mathbf{a}t') \, dt',$$

$$\mathbf{r}(t) = \mathbf{r}(0) + \mathbf{v}(0)t + \mathbf{a}t^2/2.$$

In this case the motion is neither uniform nor linear (in general). However, if the initial velocity $\mathbf{v}(0)$ is parallel to the acceleration $\mathbf{a}$ then the motion will be in a straight line. When the initial velocity $\mathbf{v}(0)$ is not parallel to the acceleration $\mathbf{a}$ the motion starts in the direction of $\mathbf{v}(0)$ and tends to the direction of $\mathbf{a}$ for long times.

Example 1.3

A particle moves in a circle with uniform angular velocity ω. In other words, the angle the radius vector makes with a fixed direction increases at the rate of ω radians per second. Obtain an expression for the velocity and acceleration.

We shall use a rectangular Cartesian system of coordinates, the motion being in the x–y plane. Then if the particle moves around the origin a distance R away, with an angular velocity ω, the position of the particle will be given by

$$\mathbf{r}(t) = x(t)\,\mathbf{i} + y(t)\,\mathbf{j}$$

where $\mathbf{i}$ and $\mathbf{j}$ are the unit vectors in the x and y directions, and we have

$$x(t) = R \cos(\omega t + \phi)$$
$$y(t) = R \sin(\omega t + \phi)$$

where ϕ is the angle that the position vector makes with the x axis at time $t = 0$. Thus

$$\mathbf{r}(t) = R\{\cos(\omega t + \phi)\,\mathbf{i} + \sin(\omega t + \phi)\,\mathbf{j}\}.$$

Differentiating with respect to time to find the velocity, we obtain

$$\mathbf{v}(t) = R\omega\{-\sin(\omega t + \phi)\,\mathbf{i} + \cos(\omega t + \phi)\,\mathbf{j}\}.$$

Differentiating once again to find the acceleration

$$\mathbf{a}(t) = -R\omega^2\{\cos(\omega t + \phi)\,\mathbf{i} + \sin(\omega t + \phi)\,\mathbf{j}\}.$$

Now, $R\{\cos(\omega t + \phi)\mathbf{i} + \sin(\omega t + \phi)\mathbf{j}\} = \mathbf{r}(t)$ so that we finally find

$$\mathbf{a}(t) = -\omega^2\mathbf{r}(t).$$

In other words the acceleration is always directed towards the centre of rotation and has a magnitude of $\omega^2 R$.

The expression for the velocity becomes self-explanatory when we write it as

$$\mathbf{v}(t) = R\omega\{\cos(\omega t + \phi + \pi/2)\mathbf{i} + \sin(\omega t + \phi + \pi/2)\mathbf{j}\}.$$

The magnitude of the velocity – the speed – is a constant $R\omega$ and the direction of the velocity is at right angles ($\pi/2$) to the radius vector, tangential to the motion.

This example demonstrates the utility of polar coordinates. To describe a general planar path in terms of polar coordinates we need to introduce unit vectors in the directions of increasing $\mathbf{r}$ and increasing ϕ. These are denoted by $\hat{\mathbf{r}}$ and $\hat{\boldsymbol{\phi}}$ and they are defined to have unit length.

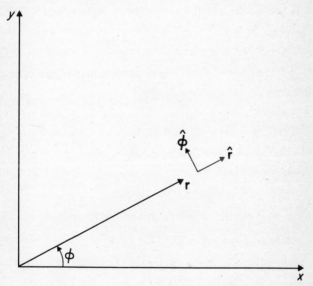

Fig. 1.3 Unit vectors in the r and ϕ direction

From Fig. 1.3 we see that they are related to the Cartesian unit vectors $\mathbf{i}$ and $\mathbf{j}$ (in the x and y directions) by

$$\hat{\mathbf{r}} = \cos\phi\,\mathbf{i} + \sin\phi\,\mathbf{j}$$
$$\hat{\boldsymbol{\phi}} = -\sin\phi\,\mathbf{i} + \cos\phi\,\mathbf{j}. \qquad [1.5]$$

Now, since we may express the position vector $\mathbf{r}$ as

$$\mathbf{r} = r\,\hat{\mathbf{r}}$$

we may simply obtain the velocity by differentiating,

$$\mathbf{v} = d\mathbf{r}/dt = \hat{\mathbf{r}}\,dr/dt + r\,d\hat{\mathbf{r}}/dt$$
$$= \hat{\mathbf{r}}\,dr/dt + r\,(d\hat{\mathbf{r}}/d\phi)\,d\phi/dt$$

but from equation [1.5]

$$d\hat{\mathbf{r}}/d\phi = \hat{\boldsymbol{\phi}}$$

so that

$$\mathbf{v} = \dot{r}\,\hat{\mathbf{r}} + r\dot{\phi}\,\hat{\boldsymbol{\phi}}. \qquad [1.6]$$

From this we can identify the radial and the angular components of the velocity v_r and v_ϕ,

$$v_r = \dot{r} \quad \text{and} \quad v_\phi = r\dot{\phi}. \qquad [1.7]$$

The acceleration components may similarly be found by differentiating the velocity,

$$\mathbf{a} = d\mathbf{v}/dt = \frac{d}{dt}(\dot{r}\,\hat{\mathbf{r}} + r\dot{\phi}\,\hat{\boldsymbol{\phi}}).$$

A little manipulation then gives

$$\mathbf{a} = (\ddot{r} - r\dot{\phi}^2)\hat{\mathbf{r}} + (r\ddot{\phi} + 2\dot{r}\dot{\phi})\hat{\boldsymbol{\phi}} \qquad [1.8]$$

so that we then have the components

$$a_r = \ddot{r} - r\dot{\phi}^2 \quad \text{and} \quad a_\phi = r\ddot{\phi} + 2\dot{r}\dot{\phi}. \qquad [1.9]$$

1.3 Newton's laws of motion

Newton set out the formulation of mechanics in 1713 in his famous book, the *Philosophiae Naturalis Principia Mathematica*. This contained various definitions, postulates, and the three laws of motion. As we have already stated, Newton's first law was simply a re-statement of Galileo's observation:

1. Every body continues in its state of rest, or uniform motion in a right line, unless it is compelled to change its state by forces impressed upon it.

This is a qualitative statement. The mathematical content comes in the second law:

2. The change of motion is proportional to the motive force impressed, and is made in the direction of the right line in which the force is impressed.

At this stage we see that the first law is simply a special case of the second law. Furthermore, the second law does not tell us anything *physical* about force. It may be taken as the definition of force, but to say how forces 'work' – the physical properties of forces – Newton introduced his third law:

3. To every action there is always opposed an equal reaction; or, the mutual actions of two bodies upon each other are always equal and directed to contrary parts.

This law contains some physics. It tells us that in a collision or other interaction between two bodies, equal but oppositely directed forces act on each.

At this stage we need precise definitions of the quantities 'motion' and 'force' that Newton uses. By motion he means something proportional to velocity, so we understand the second law to state that the rate of change of velocity is proportional to the force

$$\text{constant} \times \dot{\mathbf{v}} = \mathbf{F}.$$

This constant is peculiar to the body under investigation, and is a measure of its resistance to a change of motion by a force, i.e. its inertia. This constant is of course the mass m of the body. So we have the familiar mathematical expression of Newton's second law:

$$\mathbf{F} = m\mathbf{a}.$$

We still do not have a specification for measuring mass and force nor of defining them properly. This may be done with the aid of Newton's third law; in a collision between two bodies each will experience the same force, measured in opposite directions. The force on body 1, $\mathbf{F}_1$ is equal in magnitude and oppositely directed to the force on body 2, $\mathbf{F}_2$:

$$\mathbf{F}_1 = -\mathbf{F}_2.$$

Since the forces, and thus also the accelerations, are along the same straight line, we need only consider the magnitudes of these vectors. Using the second law

$$m_1 a_1 = -m_2 a_2$$

or

$$\frac{a_2}{a_1} = -\frac{m_1}{m_2}.$$

Thus measuring the ratio of the accelerations we know the ratio of the masses. Having specified the unit of mass, the mass of all other bodies may then be found. Once we know the mass of a body we may then use the second law for the specification of force.

Example 1.4

A diver steps off a diving board 10 m high. How long will it take for him to hit the water, and what will the velocity of impact be? (Ignore air friction.)

In problems involving fall under gravity at the earth's surface the force on a body of mass m is given by $F = mg$ where g is the acceleration due to gravity at the earth's surface, given by $g = 9.81$ m s^{-2} (in London). We have the problem of motion under a constant force, so from the second law

$$F = ma = mg$$

the acceleration being directed vertically downwards.

This then reduces to the problem of motion at constant acceleration (example 1.2), so we may quote the result

$$r(t) = r(0) + v(0)t + at^2/2.$$

Measuring the distance downwards from the diving board and denoting it by d

$$d(t) = gt^2/2.$$

(The initial velocity is zero since the diver steps off the board.) So with $g = 9.81$ m s^{-2}, the solution is the value of t for which $d(t)$ becomes 10 m. Thus

$$10 = 9.81 t^2/2$$

or

$$t = \sqrt{(20/9.81)}$$
$$= 1.43 \text{ s}.$$

The velocity of impact is given by

$$v(t) = v(0) + gt$$
$$= 0 + 9.81 \times 1.43$$
$$v = 14.03 \text{ m s}^{-1} \text{ downwards}.$$

Example 1.5

A body of mass m is attracted to a fixed point with an inverse-square-law force, $\mathbf{F} = -km/r^2 \, (\mathbf{r}/r)$, where $\mathbf{r}/r$ is a vector of unit length directed along $\mathbf{r}$. (This is a good approximation for planetary motion.) If the trajectory is a circle, verify Kepler's third law.

From example 1.3 on page 6 we know that for motion in a circle with angular velocity ω and radius r, the acceleration is directed towards the centre and given by

$$\mathbf{a} = -\omega^2 \mathbf{r}.$$

So, using Newton's second law,

$$\mathbf{F} = m\mathbf{a}$$

and substituting for $\mathbf{F}$ and $\mathbf{a}$

$$\frac{-mk}{r^2} \left(\frac{\mathbf{r}}{r}\right) = -m\omega^2 \mathbf{r}$$

or

$$k/r^3 = \omega^2.$$

Now the orbital period T is given by $2\pi/\omega$ (the time the radius vector sweeps out an angle of 2π radians), so

$$\omega = 2\pi/T$$

then $k/r^3 = (2\pi/T)^2$

or $T^2 = (2\pi)^2 r^3/k$

which is indeed Kepler's third law. We have proved the result here for the special case of a circular orbit, but of course Kepler's third law holds for the more general case of elliptical orbits once one has defined 'distance' for that case.

1.4 Galilean relativity

By the term 'frame of reference' we mean a coordinate system which we use to describe the dynamics of a body or assembly of bodies. Newton believed that there was an absolute or fixed frame of reference in terms of which all measurements should be made, but he could not identify this frame. His laws of motion in fact remain valid for a whole range of reference frames. We shall now see what these are.

Let us denote by $\mathbf{r}$ a position vector in a reference frame in which Newton's laws are valid, and let us now consider a new reference frame in which the position vector of the same point is denoted by $\mathbf{R}$. The expression for Newton's second law in the old frame is of course

$$\mathbf{F} = m\ddot{\mathbf{r}}$$

and we want to know the most general transformation such that this law of motion is valid in the new frame:

$$\mathbf{F} = m\ddot{\mathbf{R}}.$$

Subtracting these two equations, we have

$$d^2/dt^2(\mathbf{R} - \mathbf{r}) = 0.$$

This may be integrated at once,

$$d/dt(\mathbf{R} - \mathbf{r}) = \mathbf{u}, \text{ a constant}$$

and integrating again

$$\mathbf{R} - \mathbf{r} = \mathbf{u}t + \mathbf{s}$$

where **s** is another constant. We then have the expression for the vector in the new frame:

$$\mathbf{R} = \mathbf{r} + \mathbf{s} + \mathbf{u}t.$$

The arbitrary constant **s** represents a shift of the origin, a translation of vectors of the old frame by an amount **s**. The term **u**t represents the new frame moving with constant velocity **u** with respect to the old frame.

We see that Newton's laws remain unchanged if we shift the origin of our measurement system, and furthermore they remain unchanged if the new frame of reference moves with a constant velocity. The former transformation is called a translation and the latter is commonly called a boost.

The invariance of Newton's laws under translations and boosts is called Galilean invariance. This is a somewhat modern terminology introduced to contrast with the rather different invariance properties of Einstein's theory of relativity. Invariance under the above transformations is similarly referred to as Galilean relativity. Such a transformation, which preserves the form of Newton's laws, is called a Galilean transformation and we see that there is an infinity of these transformations with different **s** and **u**.

A frame of reference in which Newton's laws hold is called an *inertial* frame. There is an infinity of inertial frames, all connected by Galilean transformations.

Example 1.6

In what way do the equations of motion differ in a frame of reference that is moving with a constant acceleration **a** with respect to an inertial frame?

In this case the transformation from the old **r** to the new **R** is given by

$$\mathbf{R}(t) = \mathbf{r}(t) + \mathbf{v}t + \mathbf{a}t^2/2 \quad \text{(see example 1.2)}.$$

We know that **r**(t) obeys the equation

$$\mathbf{F} = m\ddot{\mathbf{r}}(t)$$

and **R**(t) is related to **r**(t) by

$$\ddot{\mathbf{R}}(t) = \ddot{\mathbf{r}}(t) + \mathbf{a}$$

so that

$$\mathbf{F} = m\ddot{\mathbf{r}}(t) = m[\ddot{\mathbf{R}}(t) - \mathbf{a}].$$

The equation for $\mathbf{R}(t)$ is then given by

$$(\mathbf{F} + m\mathbf{a}) = m\ddot{\mathbf{R}}.$$

In other words, in the new frame we see an extra force $m\mathbf{a}$. This is a 'fictitious' force that has appeared because we have gone into a non-inertial frame.

1.5 The formulation of Mach

It was two hundred years before a critical appraisal of Newton's laws was made (this was before quantum theory and Einstein's relativity made such a re-assessment obligatory). Ernst Mach (1838–1916) was philosopher, historian and scientist. It was this combination of talents which led him, while recognizing the gems in Newton's laws, to realize that these jewels would have far greater value when stripped of various superfluous irrelevancies.

Newton talks of mass as the 'quantity of matter' in a body and defines it as the product of density and volume. This is no help since density can only be defined as the mass of a unit volume. In the spirit of Mach, mass can be defined in terms of the dynamical equations, as we have done in section 1.3.

Newton believed in absolute space and time. In other words he believed that there was one special fixed frame of reference in terms of which everything should be described, and in terms of which his laws are valid. We have already seen in the previous section that this is all unnecessary. Any inertial frame is as good as any other.

One must separate prejudice and heartfelt belief from the scientific content of a theory, and this is precisely what Mach did. Newton had eight definitions preceding his three laws, and these were followed by six corollaries. Instead of these, Mach proposed five statements; three are experimental propositions and two are definitions.

1. *Experimental proposition*. When two bodies interact they induce in each other oppositely directed accelerations.

2. *Definition*. The mass-ratio of any two bodies is the negative inverse ratio of their mutually induced accelerations.
3. *Experimental proposition*. The mass-ratio of bodies is independent of their physical state.
4. *Experimental proposition*. The accelerations which any number of bodies induce in a body are independent of each other, i.e. forces add as vectors.
5. *Definition*. Force is defined as the product of the mass of a body and its acceleration.

These statements represent the ultimate in elegance and economy. However, at this stage a number of comments are in order.

There is a place for prejudice and heartfelt belief in the development of new theories. There they may be called scientific imagination or inspiration, but at the stage of the reasoned exposition of the new theory all unnecessary encumbrances must be removed in favour of rigorous argument—from definitions and postulates through to conclusions.

Mach believed that a theory must be formulated only in terms of observable quantities. Talk of atoms and of the discrete nature of matter was thus frowned upon, and poor Boltzmann (1844–1906), who first explored the relation between the microscopic behaviour of the atoms in a system and its macroscopic thermodynamic observable properties, committed suicide. His gravestone bears his famous formula $S = k \log W$, where S is the thermodynamic entropy of a system and W the number of atomic states compatible with the macroscopic state of the system. The world was not yet ready for that kind of 'inspiration'.

Chapter 2
Energy and momentum

2.1 Conservation laws

In principle Newton's laws are all that are necessary for the solution of dynamical problems once the forces are specified. However, there are often simpler, more subtle, ways of treating systems than the brute force application of the equations of motion. In many cases there are quantities that remain constant during the evolution of a system. If one can identify such constants of the motion, the subsequent solution of the problem may be considerably simplified. This chapter is devoted to the examination of such conserved quantities, their uses and their physical interpretation.

There is in fact a further motivation for the consideration of constants of the motion. Before embarking on a full-scale calculation for a problem, one might like to consider the following questions:

1. Does the problem have an analytic solution?
2. Do we actually want a complete analytic expression for the trajectory of the system?

If the answer to either of these questions is 'No', then we must re-think exactly what it is that we expect to get from a study of mechanics. But why might this be?

Concerning the first question, we have the surprising result that whereas the problem of two particles moving under some mutual interaction admits of an analytic solution, the problem with three of more particles does not! Approximate solutions to such problems are, then, all that can be hoped for.

Turning our attention now to the second question, consider a macroscopic system made up of some 10^{23} atoms. The solution of this dynamical problem involves the specification of over 10^{23} coordinates. Here is a different problem – there is not enough paper in the universe on which to write the solutions and, even if there were, life is too short for us to write down or read such a solution!

In these problems, where a complete analytic solution is not appropriate, one is led to the consideration of qualitative or gross descriptions of systems, for example total angular momentum or internal energy. Here, also, it is from a consideration of conserved quantities that one would start such a description.

We can understand, then, that conservation laws play a central role in mechanics, and in fact throughout the whole of physics. We shall see that conservation laws are related to symmetries of the problem under consideration. The crucial connection between symmetry and conservation laws will be treated in detail in the final chapter in section 6.4.

2 Kinetic energy and work

In this section we introduce what is probably the most important concept in physics, that of energy. We shall see that energy manifests itself in different forms and that it may be changed from one form to another. The discussion is completed in the next section when we examine the circumstances under which the total energy of a system remains constant during such transformations.

We take as our primitive concept the work done by motion in the presence of a force, and we examine the effect of this work on the subsequent motion.

When a force $\mathbf{F}$ moves a body it does work on that body. For an infinitesimal displacement $d\mathbf{r}$ the work done, dW, is the product of the force and the displacement in the direction of the force

$$dW = \mathbf{F} \cdot d\mathbf{r}. \tag{2.1}$$

Integrating this expression we may find the work done in moving the body from an initial position $\mathbf{r}_0$ to a final position $\mathbf{r}_1$

$$W = \int_{\mathbf{r}_0}^{\mathbf{r}_1} \mathbf{F} \cdot d\mathbf{r}. \qquad [2.2]$$

Now if F is the total force acting on the body we may, through Newton's second law, relate the work done to the motion, since then

$$W = m \int_{\mathbf{r}_0}^{\mathbf{r}_1} \ddot{\mathbf{r}} \cdot d\mathbf{r}. \qquad [2.3]$$

We may change the variable of integration to time by writing $d\mathbf{r}$ as $\dot{\mathbf{r}} dt$, and noting then

$$\ddot{\mathbf{r}} \cdot \dot{\mathbf{r}} = \tfrac{1}{2} \frac{d}{dt} (\dot{\mathbf{r}} \cdot \dot{\mathbf{r}}) = \tfrac{1}{2} \frac{d}{dt} \dot{\mathbf{r}}^2. \qquad [2.4]$$

This gives us

$$W = \tfrac{1}{2} m \int_{t_0}^{t_1} \frac{d}{dt} \dot{\mathbf{r}}^2 dt$$

but of course the integral and the derivative cancel each other and we are left with the result

$$W = \tfrac{1}{2} m \dot{\mathbf{r}}_1^2 - \tfrac{1}{2} m \dot{\mathbf{r}}_0^2. \qquad [2.5]$$

The work done produces an increase in the quantity $\tfrac{1}{2} m v^2$. This 'work in motion' or energy of motion is called *kinetic energy* and is given the symbol T:

$$T = \tfrac{1}{2} m v^2. \qquad [2.6]$$

The work done by the force is then given by

$$W = T - T_0. \qquad [2.7]$$

We must emphasize that this is the work done by the *total* force acting on the body. The work done by an applied force in the presence of other forces such as friction will be greater or less than that done in their absence, according to whether the other forces oppose or aid the applied force.

Example 2.1
A satellite has by mistake been put into an unstable orbit where it

is spiralling down to the earth. If the initial velocity is u when it is a distance b from the centre of the earth, find the velocity with which it will re-enter the earth's atmosphere at a distance a from the centre of the earth. We are given the constant of the motion (in fact the energy) E:

$$E = m\left(\frac{v^2}{2} - \frac{MG}{r}\right)$$

where m is the mass of the satellite, M is the mass of the earth, v is the velocity when it is a distance r from the centre of the earth, and G is a constant.

The solution is simple. The value of E evaluated from the initial condition is

$$E = m\left(\frac{u^2}{2} - \frac{MG}{b}\right)$$

and evaluated for the final condition

$$E = m\left(\frac{v^2}{2} - \frac{MG}{a}\right).$$

So equating these we find the final velocity v to be

$$v = \left\{u^2 + 2GM\left(\frac{1}{a} - \frac{1}{b}\right)\right\}^{\frac{1}{2}}.$$

It is clear that the effort involved in solving this problem is considerably less than the working through of Newton's laws.

3 Conservative forces

The work done in moving from one point $\mathbf{r}_0$ to another $\mathbf{r}_1$ in the presence of a force $\mathbf{F}$ is, in general, dependent on the path taken. Mathematically the value of this work W is given by the line integral

$$W = \int_{\mathbf{r}_0}^{\mathbf{r}_1} \mathbf{F} \cdot d\mathbf{r}$$

which depends, in general, on the path of integration. Further, if the force depends on the velocity, then the work done will depend on the time behaviour of the trajectory as well.

However, many of the forces of nature have the important property that the work done does *not* depend on the path but only on the end points. Such forces are known as *conservative* forces.

Given an arbitrary reference point $\mathbf{r}_0$, the work that would be done in going from a general point $\mathbf{r}$ to the reference point is a unique (scalar) function of the position $\mathbf{r}$ for a conservative force. Each point in space may then be characterized by a particular value of this 'potential work', or *potential energy* as it is known. It is given the symbol V:

$$V(\mathbf{r}) = \int_{\mathbf{r}}^{\mathbf{r}_0} \mathbf{F} \cdot d\mathbf{r}. \qquad [2.8]$$

It is only when $\mathbf{F}$ is conservative that $V(\mathbf{r})$ is a unique function of $\mathbf{r}$. There is of course always an additional constant associated with V, determined by the reference point $\mathbf{r}_0$, and this is normally chosen to simplify the problem in hand.

We may look at the condition that a force is conservative in a slightly different way. If the work done in going between two points is independent of path, consider two paths A and B (see Fig. 2.1).

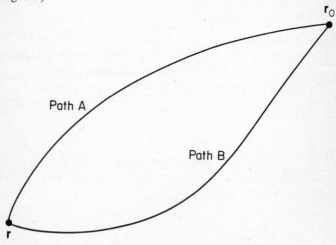

Fig. 2.1 Two paths joining $\mathbf{r}$ and $\mathbf{r}_0$

For a conservative force

$$\int_{\mathbf{r}}^{\mathbf{r}_0} \mathbf{F} \cdot d\mathbf{r} = \int_{\mathbf{r}}^{\mathbf{r}_0} \mathbf{F} \cdot d\mathbf{r}$$
Path A   Path B

or

$$\int_{\mathbf{r}}^{\mathbf{r}_0} \mathbf{F} \cdot d\mathbf{r} - \int_{\mathbf{r}}^{\mathbf{r}_0} \mathbf{F} \cdot d\mathbf{r} = 0.$$
Path A   Path B

Now, inverting the limits of the second integral

$$\int_{\mathbf{r}}^{\mathbf{r}_0} \mathbf{F} \cdot d\mathbf{r} + \int_{\mathbf{r}_0}^{\mathbf{r}} \mathbf{F} \cdot d\mathbf{r} = 0.$$
Path A   Path B

But these two integrals together describe the closed path from $\mathbf{r}$ to $\mathbf{r}_0$ along A and return to $\mathbf{r}$ along B.

$$\oint \mathbf{F} \cdot d\mathbf{r} = 0. \tag{2.9}$$

In other words, around a closed loop the line integral is zero — an equivalent definition for a conservative force.

The line integral of a vector around a loop divided by the surface area of the loop is, in the limit of an infinitesimally small loop, given by the curl of the vector. So from equation [2.9] we have

$$\text{curl } \mathbf{F} = 0. \tag{2.10}$$

This may be regarded as a differential expression for $\mathbf{F}$, since the curl may be expressed as a differential operation given by the determinant mnemonic

$$\text{curl } \mathbf{F} = \begin{pmatrix} \mathbf{i} & \mathbf{j} & \mathbf{k} \\ \partial/\partial x & \partial/\partial y & \partial/\partial z \\ F_x & F_y & F_z \end{pmatrix}$$

Example 2.2

Are the following forces conservative:

1. $\mathbf{F}(\mathbf{r}) = \mathbf{a}$
2. $\mathbf{F}(\mathbf{r}) = a\mathbf{r}$
3. $\mathbf{F}(\mathbf{r}) = a\,(\mathbf{i}y + 2\mathbf{j}x)$
4. $\mathbf{F}(\mathbf{r}) = \mathbf{a} \times \mathbf{r}$

where a is a constant scalar and $\mathbf{a}$ is a constant vector?

1. Curl $\mathbf{F}$ = curl $\mathbf{a}$ = 0, since $\mathbf{a}$ is constant. Thus this force is conservative.
2. Curl $\mathbf{F}$ = a curl $\mathbf{r}$ = 0, since $\partial x/\partial y$, etc. = 0. Thus this force is also conservative.
3. Let us evaluate the z component of the curl:

$$\text{curl } \mathbf{F}|_z = \frac{\partial F_y}{\partial x} - \frac{\partial F_x}{\partial y}.$$

   Since $F_x = ay$, $F_y = 2ax$, we have curl $\mathbf{F}|_z = a \neq 0$. This force is not conservative.
4. Curl $\mathbf{F}$ = curl $(\mathbf{a} \times \mathbf{r})$ = $2\mathbf{a}$, which may be evaluated by direct differentiation. As the curl is non-zero this force is also not conservative.

Let us now see why these forces are called conservative forces. Recall that in section 2.2 we saw that the work done could be expressed as the difference between the initial and final kinetic energies (equation [2.7]):

$$W = \int_{\mathbf{r}_0}^{\mathbf{r}_1} \mathbf{F} \cdot d\mathbf{r} = T_1 - T_0 \qquad [2.11]$$

where T is given by $\frac{1}{2}mv^2$. For a conservative force we may write the work done in terms of the potential energy at the end points:

$$\int_{\mathbf{r}_0}^{\mathbf{r}_1} \mathbf{F} \cdot d\mathbf{r} = \int_{\mathbf{r}_0}^{\text{ref. pt}} \mathbf{F} \cdot d\mathbf{r} - \int_{\mathbf{r}_1}^{\text{ref. pt}} \mathbf{F} \cdot d\mathbf{r}$$

$$= V(\mathbf{r}_0) - V(\mathbf{r}_1)$$

or $$= V_0 - V_1$$

which, considered with equation [2.11], gives

$$T_1 - T_0 = V_0 - V_1$$

or

$$T_0 + V_0 = T_1 + V_1.$$

[2.12]

Now the final point $\mathbf{r}_1$ may be taken as any point on the trajectory, so that we have the result that the sum of the kinetic energy and the potential energy is a constant throughout the motion:

$$T + V = E, \text{a constant.}$$

[2.13]

Energy is conserved in the presence of what we have called a conservative force.

Finally, given the potential energy as a function of position, the question arises, Can we invert equation [2.8] to find the force? The difference in potential energy between two points infinitesimally close together is given by

$$dV = V(\mathbf{r} + d\mathbf{r}) - V(\mathbf{r})$$

$$= \int_{\mathbf{r}+d\mathbf{r}}^{\mathbf{r}_0} \mathbf{F} \cdot d\mathbf{r} - \int_{\mathbf{r}}^{\mathbf{r}_0} \mathbf{F} \cdot d\mathbf{r}$$

$$= - \mathbf{F} \cdot d\mathbf{r}.$$

For simplicity, let us express this in rectangular Cartesian components:

$$dV = -(F_x dx + F_y dy + F_z dz).$$

Now we can identify the partial derivatives:

$$F_x = -\partial V/\partial x$$
$$F_y = -\partial V/\partial y$$
$$F_z = -\partial V/\partial z$$

[2.14]

or, putting these together

$$\mathbf{F} = -\left(\frac{\partial V}{\partial x}\mathbf{i} + \frac{\partial V}{\partial y}\mathbf{j} + \frac{\partial V}{\partial z}\mathbf{k}\right)$$

[2.15]

which is simply the definition of the gradient of the scalar V:

$$\mathbf{F} = -\text{grad } V. \qquad\qquad [2.16]$$

The force may thus be expressed as the negative gradient of the potential energy. We have already seen that curl $\mathbf{F} = 0$ for a conservative force equation [2.10]. This is in conformity with equation [2.16] since, taking the curl,

$$\text{curl } \mathbf{F} = -\text{curl grad } V = 0$$

since curl grad is identically zero.

Example 2.3

Two forces which depend on velocity are friction and the magnetic force. The force of friction is in the opposite direction to the velocity of motion and is approximately proportional to the velocity $\mathbf{v}$.

$$\mathbf{F} = -\gamma\mathbf{v}.$$

The force on a charge Q in a magnetic field $\mathbf{B}$ is given by the Lorentz force:

$$\mathbf{F} = Q\mathbf{v} \times \mathbf{B}.$$

Are these forces conservative?

Let us evaluate the work done in traversing a closed loop. To overcome the force of friction and achieve a velocity $\mathbf{v}$ we must apply a force $\mathbf{F} = \gamma\mathbf{v}$, so that the work done in traversing a path is given by

$$W = \int \mathbf{F} \cdot d\mathbf{x} = \gamma \int \mathbf{v} \cdot d\mathbf{x}$$

with

$$d\mathbf{x} = (d\mathbf{x}/dt)\ dt = \mathbf{v}\ dt$$

so that

$$W = \gamma \int v^2\, dt$$

and this is always greater than zero unless the velocity is zero, in which case one cannot traverse the path. The work done in covering any path, closed or otherwise, is always positive. The frictional force is thus certainly not conservative.

Now let us look at the magnetic force on a charge in a magnetic field. To overcome the force of the field on the charge we must apply a force $\mathbf{F} = Q\mathbf{B} \times \mathbf{v}$. The work done is then

$$W = Q\int \mathbf{B} \times \mathbf{v} \cdot d\mathbf{x}$$
$$= Q\int \mathbf{B} \times \mathbf{v} \cdot \mathbf{v}dt.$$

Permuting operations within the triple product

$$W = Q\int \mathbf{B} \cdot \mathbf{v} \times \mathbf{v} \, dt = 0$$

since $\mathbf{v} \times \mathbf{v} = 0$. The work done against a magnetic force is always zero! In fact this is hardly surprising since the force is always perpendicular to the motion and so cannot affect the energy. The magnetic force, then, is conservative.

Looked at from another point of view, however, this is all a little unfortunate. The potential energy of a charged particle in a magnetic field is always zero, so the magnetic force cannot be expressed as the gradient of a potential energy function. Until we reach section 6.6 we must be content with treating the magnetic force explicitly in terms of the Lorentz force formula.

We have seen in this section that under certain circumstances the sum of kinetic energy and potential energy is a constant. This is a simple example of the principle of conservation of energy. One of the required circumstances is that the force be expressed as the gradient of a scalar function of position, and this puts quite a restriction on the sorts of force allowed since they are related to one independent number at each point, rather than three.

Energy conservation is, however, rather more general than this. When a system appears not to conserve energy, we are able to introduce other manifestations of energy without producing contradictions such that total energy remains conserved. Thus friction involves the loss of energy from a system to its environment. The energy of the system plus environment remains constant. In this case, to simplify the treatment of the environment, one introduces the idea of heat energy. Friction will be discussed in greater detail in section 4.5.

Example 2.4

A man is doing a pole vault. What is the sequence of energy conversions? If he jumps a height of 5 m how fast must he be running before he takes off?

The energy sequence is chemical energy in his body, kinetic energy of his motion while running, potential energy in the pole while it is bent, kinetic energy as he jumps up, potential energy at the top of the flight due to gravity, kinetic energy as he hits the ground, heat energy after impact.

If his weight is m then the potential energy at the top of his flight of height h is mgh. This must come from his kinetic energy before take-off, i.e. $\frac{1}{2}mv^2$. So we have

$$\frac{1}{2}mv^2 = mgh$$

or
$$\begin{aligned} v &= \sqrt{(2gh)} \\ &= \sqrt{(2 \times 9.81 \times 5)} \\ &= 9.9 \text{ m s}^{-1}. \end{aligned}$$

This must be his initial velocity (but one can jump from rest!)

2.4 Momentum and momentum conservation

Another quantity often conserved in physical systems is the vector quantity momentum. The linear momentum of a body is given by the product of its mass m and its velocity $\mathbf{v}$, and it is usually given the symbol $\mathbf{p}$:

$$\mathbf{p} = m\mathbf{v}. \qquad [2.17]$$

In terms of momentum, Newton's second law takes the particularly simple form:

$$\dot{\mathbf{p}} = \mathbf{F} \qquad [2.18]$$

i.e. the rate of change of momentum of a body is equal to the force impressed.

If we now consider the case of no force we see that $\dot{\mathbf{p}} = 0$, or

$$\mathbf{p} = \text{constant}. \qquad [2.19]$$

In the absence of force the momentum of a body is a constant. This is the law of conservation of momentum.

It is important to appreciate the vectorial nature of this conservation law. We have, in fact, three laws—one for each component. In other words, if the force is zero in a particular direction then the component of momentum in that direction is a constant. It may thus be advantageous to choose the coordinate system to reflect any symmetry of the impressed force.

A further example of momentum conservation relates to two (or more) bodies with mutual interactions obeying Newton's third law. Let us take two bodies of momentum $\mathbf{p}_1$ and $\mathbf{p}_2$, and let them interact with a mutual force. Newton's third law tells us that if body 1 experiences a force $\mathbf{F}$ then body 2 experiences a force $-\mathbf{F}$. Newton's second law then takes the form

$$\dot{\mathbf{p}}_1 = \mathbf{F}, \qquad \dot{\mathbf{p}}_2 = -\mathbf{F}.$$

Adding these equations

$$\dot{\mathbf{p}}_1 + \dot{\mathbf{p}}_2 = 0$$

or, on integrating,

$$\mathbf{p}_1 + \mathbf{p}_2 = \text{constant}.$$

In any interaction which obeys Newton's third law we see that the total momentum is a constant of the motion. Clearly the result can be generalized to any number of particles, as will be done in section 4.1.

Example 2.5

Consider a collision between two spheres of identical mass, one sphere initially at rest.
1. Show that after the collision the two velocity vectors will be at right angles to each other.
2. Show that for head-on collision the moving sphere is brought to rest.

Conservation of energy and momentum are assumed.

For 1 we only need energy conservation. Let $\mathbf{u}$ be the initial velocity and $\mathbf{v}_1$ and $\mathbf{v}_2$ the final velocities of the spheres. Then

$$\tfrac{1}{2}mu^2 = \tfrac{1}{2}mv_1^2 + \tfrac{1}{2}mv_2^2$$

or

$$u^2 = v_1^2 + v_2^2$$

But by Pythagoras's theorem we then know that lines of length u, v_1, v_2 form a right-angled triangle. The vectors $\mathbf{v}_1$ and $\mathbf{v}_2$ are therefore perpendicular.

Considering now the head-on collision, all velocities may be measured along the same line. Energy and momentum conservation then give the equations

$$u^2 = v_1^2 + v_2^2$$
$$u = v_1 + v_2.$$

Squaring the second equation and subtracting the first we find $v_1 v_2 = 0$, so that $v_1 = 0$ or $v_2 = 0$. After the collision it must be the rear sphere that is stationary and the front one that moves with the original velocity of the incident sphere.

2.5 Angular momentum

We have seen that for each component of force that is zero, the corresponding component of the momentum is conserved. The question then arises as to whether the idea of a component of a vector can be extended to non-Cartesian components (for instance, polar coordinates). Such a question has relevance if the force field has a particular symmetry (such as a central force). It turns out that one can indeed consider non-Cartesian components and the full generality of this is explored in chapter 6. For the moment we shall simply treat the concept of angular momentum in a relatively naive way by developing the rotational analogue of Newton's second law.

We have seen that the second law may be expressed simply in terms of linear momentum $\mathbf{p} = m\mathbf{v}$:

$$\dot{\mathbf{p}} = \mathbf{F}.$$

The rotational analogue is obtained by taking the cross product with the displacement vector $\mathbf{r}$:

$$\mathbf{r} \times \dot{\mathbf{p}} = \mathbf{r} \times \mathbf{F}.$$

But $\mathbf{r} \times \dot{\mathbf{p}} = d/dt(\mathbf{r} \times \mathbf{p})$

since

$$\dot{\mathbf{r}} \times \mathbf{p} = \mathbf{v} \times m\mathbf{v} = 0.$$

The equation of motion is then $\dfrac{d}{dt} (\mathbf{r} \times \mathbf{p}) = \mathbf{r} \times \mathbf{F}$

$$[2.20]$$

which we may compare with $\dfrac{d\mathbf{p}}{dt} = \mathbf{F}$.

Instead of the rate of change of momentum being given by the force, in equation [2.20] we see that the rate of change of 'rotational momentum', $\mathbf{r} \times \mathbf{p}$, is given by the 'rotational force' $\mathbf{r} \times \mathbf{F}$.

The 'rotational force' we see is the moment of the force about the origin. We call this vector the *torque* and give it the symbol $\mathbf{N}$:

$$\mathbf{N} = \mathbf{r} \times \mathbf{F}. \qquad [2.21]$$

The 'rotational momentum' is more commonly known as the *angular momentum* and is given the symbol $\mathbf{L}$:

$$\mathbf{L} = \mathbf{r} \times \mathbf{p}. \qquad [2.22]$$

In terms of these new quantities we may write the rotational equation of motion as

$$\dot{\mathbf{L}} = \mathbf{N} \qquad [2.23]$$

i.e. the rate of change of angular momentum is equal to the applied torque.

Example 2.6

A particle of mass m is moving in a plane and its position is specified in terms of the plane polar coordinates r, ϕ. Express the angular momentum in terms of these variables.

Let the plane of motion be the x-y plane. Then the position of the particle may be expressed as

$$\mathbf{r} = r(\cos \phi\, \mathbf{i} + \sin \phi\, \mathbf{j})$$

and the momentum is then

$$\mathbf{p} = m\dot{\mathbf{r}} = mr\dot{\phi}(-\sin \phi\, \mathbf{i} + \cos \phi\, \mathbf{j}).$$

Expressing the cross product in terms of the conveniently remembered determinant mnemonic:

$$L = r \times p = \begin{pmatrix} i & j & k \\ x & y & z \\ p_x & p_y & p_z \end{pmatrix}$$

$$= \begin{pmatrix} i & j & k \\ r\cos\phi & r\sin\phi & 0 \\ -mr\dot\phi\sin\phi & mr\dot\phi\cos\phi & 0 \end{pmatrix}$$

and on multiplying this out we obtain

$$L = mr^2\dot\phi k.$$

The angular momentum has magnitude $mr^2\dot\phi$ and direction normal to the plane of motion.

We have seen that momentum is conserved in the absence of force. From equation [2.23] we can draw the corresponding conclusion for the rotational case – angular momentum is conserved in the absence of torque.

Of course a special case of this is where there is no force, i.e. the angular momentum of a free particle about an arbitrary point is a constant. However, a rather more general case is that of a central force, of which gravitation and the Coulomb force are examples.

A central force is always directed towards (or away from) a fixed point and its magnitude depends only on the distance from this point. Taking the force centre as the origin we may write the force as

$$F(r) = f(r)\hat{r}$$

where $\hat{r}$ is a vector in the direction of r, having unit length. The torque is obtained by taking the cross-product with r,

$$N = r \times F = f(r) r \times \hat{r}$$

$$= 0.$$

The torque for a central force is zero, so that the angular momentum is conserved.

This is a nice example of a symmetry leading to a conservation law. The rotational symmetry implies the conservation of angular momentum.

Chapter 3
Dynamics of a single particle

The general problem treated in this chapter is the solution of the dynamics of a single particle once the force field is specified. In most cases, since we shall be dealing with conservative systems, the force will be obtained from a potential energy function.

In the spirit of the discussion at the start of chapter 2, concerning the existence and desirability of analytic solutions, we shall commence with an examination of the qualitative features of solutions. We will base this on a consideration of only the gross features of the force or potential energy. For simplicity we shall start with motion in one dimension. This will then set the scene for the general case, treated in later sections.

3.1 One-dimensional motion

The kinetic energy and potential energy functions are very different objects. Whereas we know that the kinetic energy is always given by $\frac{1}{2}mv^2$, we may not know the form of the potential energy function — it is that which specifies the problem. However, we can already draw a number of conclusions.

The v^2 term in the kinetic energy tells us that it can never be negative, so from the energy conservation expression

$$T + V = E$$

the condition that T is greater than or equal to zero

$$T \geqslant 0$$

then implies that V must be less than or equal to the total energy E:

$$V \leqslant E. \qquad\qquad\qquad [3.1]$$

Assuming that the potential energy is a function of position alone, what this inequality is telling us is that only those regions of space for which $V(x) \leqslant E$ are accessible for the motion. There are three qualitatively different sorts of motion, as shown in Fig. 3.1 for the energies E_1, E_2, E_3.

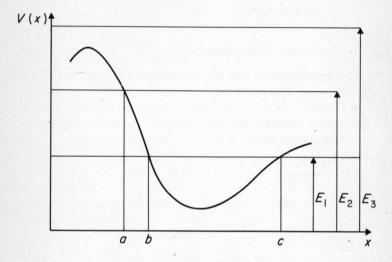

Fig. 3.1 Typical potential energy function

For energy E_1 the inequality [3.1] is satisfied only for the values of x:

$$b \leqslant x \leqslant c.$$

The motion is said to be *bounded*. Furthermore, at the boundaries b and c, since there $V = E$, the kinetic energy and hence the velocity is zero. The motion then is oscillatory between these two turning points.

For somewhat greater energy E_2 there is still a boundary when the potential energy is sufficiently large, and there is a turning point on the left at $x = a$. There is no boundary on the right, however, since there the total energy always exceeds the potential energy. The allowed values of x are then

$$a \leqslant x \leqslant \infty$$

and motion to the left always results in reflection at the turning point.

Finally for even greater energy E_3 there are no turning points. The motion always continues in the same direction and all regions of space are accessible:

$$-\infty \leqslant x \leqslant \infty.$$

3.2 General solution of one-dimensional motion

One-dimensional motion has the important property that it can always be solved in terms of a single integral, so no matter how complicated the potential energy, the trajectory may be found, at worst, by numerical integration. We may see this from the energy-conservation equation, which we write in the form

$$\tfrac{1}{2}m\dot{x}^2 + V(x) = E.$$

This may be solved for $\dot{x}$:

$$\dot{x} = \frac{dx}{dt} = \left[\frac{2}{m} \{E - V(x)\} \right]^{\frac{1}{2}}$$

so that

$$\frac{dt}{dx} = \left(\frac{m}{2}\right)^{\frac{1}{2}} \frac{1}{\{E - V(x)\}^{\frac{1}{2}}}.$$

We can now integrate with respect to x, giving

$$t(x) = t(x_0) + \left(\frac{m}{2}\right)^{\frac{1}{2}} \int_{x_0}^{x} \frac{dx}{\{E - V(x)\}^{\frac{1}{2}}}. \qquad [3.2]$$

Upon integration, then, we have the time the particle passes through each point, i.e. the trajectory. True, one may prefer the inverse function $x(t)$, but the point to note is that the problem always admits of a solution by quadrature (simple integration). Systems of more than one dimension do not generally permit solution in this way.

3.3 Harmonic motion – small oscillations

Simple harmonic, or sinusoidal, motion has a central position in physics. The force producing such motion is one proportional to, and opposing, the displacement, in other words Hooke's law. In this section we shall examine the reasons for the ubiquity of this particular type of motion.

We are interested in bounded motion, so let us look at Fig. 3.2, which shows the sort of potential energy function we are dealing with.

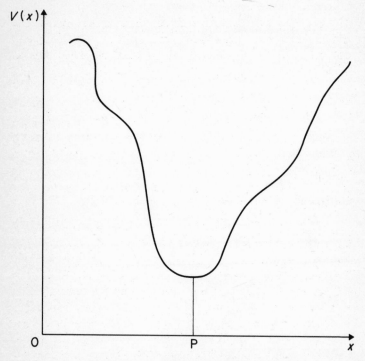

Fig. 3.2 Potential energy for bound motion

The minimum point P is of particular importance. Recall that one obtains the force from the potential energy by differentiation:

$$F = -\frac{dV}{dx} \qquad [3.3]$$

34   *Classical mechanics*

so where the slope of V is zero there is no force. A particle placed at rest at this point will stay there. This is a point of equilibrium.

In this section we shall study the sort of motion that occurs in the neighbourhood of such points. To this end we shall choose a new coordinate origin at the equilibrium point P. For relatively small departures from equilibrium we may develop $V(x)$ in a Taylor series about equilibrium:

$$V(x) = V(0) + \frac{dV}{dx}\bigg|_0 x + \frac{d^2V}{dx^2}\bigg|_0 \frac{x^2}{2!} + \dots . \qquad [3.4]$$

The first term is a constant and may therefore be ignored. The second term is zero since dV/dx vanishes at the equilibrium point. The third term is then the lowest-order non-vanishing term, so defining the force constant k by

$$k = \frac{d^2V}{dx^2}\bigg|_0, \qquad [3.5]$$

for small displacement x, the potential energy function has the parabolic form

$$V(x) = \tfrac{1}{2}kx^2. \qquad [3.6]$$

Differentiating to find the force, we obtain

$$F(x) = -kx \qquad [3.7]$$

and we have recovered Hooke's law.

This relies on $k = d^2V/dx^2$ being positive, in other words, a minimum in V. Now for a general stationary point of V, when its first derivative vanishes, the second derivative may be positive, zero, or negative. When it is positive a small displacement results in a force *towards* the equilibrium point—a restoring force. This, then, is a point of stable equilibrium. If, conversely, the second derivative were negative—a maximum in V—a small displacement would result in a force away from the equilibrium point, resulting in unstable equilibrium. When the second derivative is zero one must examine the higher derivatives to characterize the equilibrium.

To solve the problem of small oscillations about equilibrium, we can write down Newton's law

$$-kx = m\ddot{x} \qquad [3.8]$$

or

$$\ddot{x} + \frac{k}{m}x = 0, \qquad [3.8]$$

a second-order homogeneous differential equation. The general solution is given by

$$x(t) = A \cos \omega t + B \sin \omega t \qquad [3.9]$$

where the angular frequency ω can be found by direct substitution into the equation of motion:

$$\omega^2 = \frac{k}{m} \qquad [3.10]$$

corresponding to a period of

$$T = \frac{2\pi}{\omega}$$

or

$$T = 2\pi \left(\frac{m}{k}\right)^{\frac{1}{2}}. \qquad [3.11]$$

We recognize this solution as simple harmonic motion. The nature of the motion is independent of the precise form of the potential energy, and this explains the appearance of harmonic oscillation in so many different areas of physics.

Example 3.1

What is the period of small oscillations in a sinusoidal potential $V = V_0 \sin ax$?

An equilibrium point is at $-ax = \pi/2$. Thus using the variable y to denote displacements from the position $x = \pi/2a + y$, we may expand the potential in powers of y:

$$V = V_0 \sin (ay - \pi/2)$$
$$= -V_0 \cos ay$$
$$= V_0 \left(-1 + \frac{a^2 y^2}{2!} + \dots \right).$$

Differentiating twice we obtain

$$\left.\frac{d^2 V}{dy^2}\right|_0 = V_0 a^2$$

which is equal to the k of equation [3.5]. Thus the period is then given by

$$T = \frac{2\pi}{a}\left(\frac{m}{V_0}\right)^{1/2}.$$

Example 3.2

Obtain and solve the equation of motion for a simple pendulum, mass m, length l, executing small oscillations.

In terms of the angular variable ϕ the kinetic energy is $\frac{1}{2}ml^2\dot{\phi}^2$ and the potential energy is $-mgl\cos\phi$, measured with respect to the point of support. Energy conservation then gives

$$\tfrac{1}{2}ml^2\dot{\phi}^2 - mgl\cos\phi = E.$$

Differentiating with respect to time we find the usual equation of motion:

$$\ddot{\phi} + \frac{g}{l}\sin\phi = 0.$$

For small ϕ we expand the sine:

$$\ddot{\phi} + \frac{g}{l}\left(\phi - \frac{\phi^2}{2!}\ldots\right) = 0.$$

Keeping only the linear term, we can solve for

$$\phi(t) = A\cos\omega t + B\sin\omega t$$

where

$$\omega = \left(\frac{g}{l}\right)^{1/2}$$

the familiar result.

3.4 Central forces

We now turn our attention to the study of motion under a central force. We saw in section 2.5 that such a force is given by an expression of the form

$$\mathbf{F}(\mathbf{r}) = f(r)\,\hat{\mathbf{r}} \qquad [3.12]$$

and that the angular momentum

$$\mathbf{L} = \mathbf{r} \times \mathbf{p} \qquad [3.13]$$

is conserved in the presence of this force.

Conservation of angular momentum has the important consequence that the motion occurs in a plane. Establishment of this feature then enables us to simplify the choice of coordinates used when we set up the equations of motion. From the definition of angular momentum we see that $\mathbf{r}$ is perpendicular to $\mathbf{L}$. When angular momentum is conserved the position vector is always perpendicular to a constant vector. Thus throughout the motion, $\mathbf{r}$ remains in the plane perpendicular to the constant vector $\mathbf{L}$. The problem of motion under a central force reduces, then, to a problem in two dimensions and the mathematics is considerably simplified.

We now proceed to the equations governing such motion. It can be shown that a central force is conservative and derivable from a potential energy function $V(r)$ (see exercise 3, chapter 2, Appendix 1). Thus we may discuss the motion directly in terms of energy. We shall use plane polar coordinates r, ϕ and, using the result of exercise 5, chapter 2 (Appendix 1), we write the kinetic energy as

$$T = \frac{\mu}{2}(\dot{r}^2 + r^2\dot{\phi}^2). \qquad [3.14]$$

(We are denoting the mass of the particle by μ for reasons that will become apparent in section 4.2.)

Energy conservation gives us the equation

$$\frac{\mu}{2}(\dot{r}^2 + r^2\dot{\phi}^2) + V(r) = E. \qquad [3.15]$$

This is a partial differential equation in r and ϕ. We also have conservation of angular momentum $L = \mu r^2 \dot{\phi}$. Elimination of $\dot{\phi}$ from the energy equation gives an ordinary differential equation which can always be solved by integration. Luckily this elimination can be done in terms of the angular momentum:

$$L = \mu r^2 \dot{\phi}$$

since then

$$\dot{\phi} = L/\mu r^2 \qquad [3.16]$$

and the energy equation may then be written as

$$\tfrac{1}{2}\mu\dot{r}^2 + \frac{L^2}{2\mu r^2} + V(r) = E. \qquad [3.17]$$

Now this equation has a rather interesting interpretation. It describes a particle executing one-dimensional motion in an effective potential $V'(r)$ where

$$V'(r) = V(r) + \frac{L^2}{2\mu r^2}. \qquad [3.18]$$

The extra term, $L^2/2\mu r^2$, is known as the *centrifugal potential energy*. It gives a force which is repulsive, away from the force centre.

The integration of equation [3.17] proceeds as for the case of one-dimensional motion treated in section 3.2: we simply substitute $V'(r)$ for $V(x)$ in equation [3.2]:

$$t(r) = \left(\frac{\mu}{2}\right)^{\tfrac{1}{2}} \int \frac{\mathrm{d}r}{\{E - V(r) - L^2/2\mu r^2\}^{\tfrac{1}{2}}}. \qquad [3.19]$$

Having evaluated this integral one may then use the angular momentum to find the angle ϕ and the problem is solved. This rather formal treatment shows that one can always solve the problem of motion under any central force.

Alternatively (and more probably), one may prefer to solve directly for the shape of the orbit, the functional relation between r and ϕ. This may be done by eliminating $\mathrm{d}r/\mathrm{d}t$ in favour of $\mathrm{d}r/\mathrm{d}\phi$ in the following way. We use the chain-rule expression:

$$\frac{\mathrm{d}r}{\mathrm{d}t} = \frac{\mathrm{d}r}{\mathrm{d}\phi}\frac{\mathrm{d}\phi}{\mathrm{d}t}$$

and from the definition of angular momentum we have

$$\frac{\mathrm{d}\phi}{\mathrm{d}t} = L/\mu r^2$$

so that

$$\frac{\mathrm{d}r}{\mathrm{d}t} = \frac{\mathrm{d}r}{\mathrm{d}\phi} \frac{L}{\mu r^2} .$$

Substituting this into equation [3.17], the differential equation for the orbit is

$$\frac{L^2}{2\mu r^2} \left\{ \frac{1}{r^2} \left(\frac{\mathrm{d}r}{\mathrm{d}\phi} \right)^2 + 1 \right\} + V(r) = E. \qquad [3.20]$$

This may be integrated, giving ϕ as a function of r:

$$\phi = \int r^{-2} \frac{\mathrm{d}r}{\left[\frac{2\mu}{L^2} \{E - V(r)\} - \frac{1}{r^2} \right]^{1/2}} \qquad [3.21]$$

and this expression describes the shape of the orbit, the relation between the angular coordinate ϕ and the radial variable r.

3.5 Qualitative features of motion under a central force

We have obtained, in section 3.4, the complete solution to the problem of motion under a central force. The shape of the orbit is given in equation [3.21] and the temporal behaviour in equation [3.19]. In the general case these integrals are complicated and they may not be expressed in terms of the elementary functions. This complexity can obscure the essential features of the motion, so we pause at this point to see what qualitative conclusion can be drawn.

Recall that the equation for radial motion (equation [3.17]) had a quasi one-dimensional form, representing motion under an effective potential $V'(r)$ (equation [3.18])

$$\tfrac{1}{2}\mu\dot{r}^2 + V'(r) = E$$

where from equation [3.18]

$$V'(r) = V(r) + L^2/2\mu r^2 .$$

Consideration of these equations will enable us to see whether the motion is bounded or unbounded and whether the particle can fall into the force centre or not.

The requirement that $\dot{r}^2$ is positive immediately gives those values of r that are allowed; they are the values that satisfy the inequality

$$E \geqslant V(r) + L^2/2\mu r^2, \qquad [3.22]$$

equality occurring at the end points.

Bound motion occurs when one has an attractive potential, $\mathrm{d}V/\mathrm{d}r > 0$, and the effective potential has a minimum.

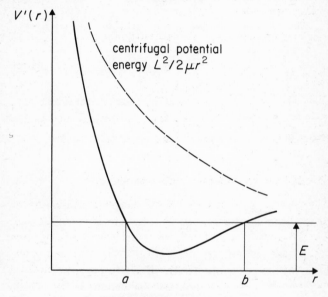

Fig. 3.3 Motion under a central force

We have a 'radial oscillation' in the well between the extreme points a and b (see Fig. 3.3). For larger energy E, then $b \to \infty$ and the particle can go off to infinity. Then the motion ceases to be bound. We also see that if the energy E is just the minimum of the effective potential, then r is a constant and we have circular motion.

Example 3.3

Show that for a central potential of the form $V(r) = -k/r$ the path will be a circle when the energy has the value

$$E = -\frac{\mu k^2}{2L^2}.$$

The motion is circular when the energy is equal to the minimum value of the effective potential energy. In this case

$$V'(r) = \frac{L^2}{2\mu r^2} - \frac{k}{r}.$$

To find the minimum we differentiate this and set it equal to zero:

$$\frac{dV'}{dr} = -\frac{L^2}{\mu r^3} + \frac{k}{r^2} = 0$$

from which we solve for the radius of the circular orbit

$$r_0 = \frac{L^2}{\mu k}.$$

The energy is then given by

$$E = \frac{L^2}{2\mu r_0^2} - \frac{k}{r_0}$$

$$= -\frac{\mu k^2}{2L^2}.$$

For a repulsive potential $dV/dr < 0$, and this form of force will be further reinforced by the repulsive nature of the centrifugal potential energy. The one value of r that satisfies the equality of equation [3.22] then gives the distance of closest approach.

3.6 The Kepler problem

Both the gravitational and the electrostatic interaction are central forces with an inverse square law. These are the most common of the elementary forces of nature and their solutions are clearly similar. Since Kepler did so much work on the gravitational force, the general problem of the inverse-square-law force is known as the Kepler problem.

Of course we have all the solutions in the equations of section 3.4; substitution of the correct form for $V(r)$ followed by integration is all that is required. However, the inverse-square-law force has other special features, apart from being so common. Bound motion under this force has the peculiar feature that the orbit is a closed curve — the orientation in space of the orbit is constant. This may be treated in terms of a further conserved quantity known as the Runge–Lenz vector which specifies the orientation and shape of the orbit, as we shall see. It is related to the other constants of the motion, energy and angular momenta, but the use of this extra constant of the motion presents a straightforward solution of the system.

We shall write the potential energy of the general inverse-square-law problem as

$$V(r) = -\frac{k}{r} \qquad [3.23]$$

where k is positive for attraction and negative for repulsion. Upon differentiation this gives the required force (since $F = -\text{grad } V(r)$):

$$\mathbf{F} = -\frac{k}{r^2}\frac{\mathbf{r}}{r} = -\frac{k\mathbf{r}}{r^3}. \qquad [3.24]$$

We now define the Runge–Lenz vector $\mathbf{A}$:

$$\mathbf{A} = \mathbf{p} \times \mathbf{L} - \mu k \frac{\mathbf{r}}{r} \qquad [3.25]$$

which may be regarded as $\mathbf{p} \times \mathbf{L}$ plus something else such that the sum is constant. We shall show that $\mathbf{A}$ is constant for the inverse-square-law force by demonstrating that its derivative with respect to time is zero. Differentiating:

$$\dot{\mathbf{A}} = \dot{\mathbf{p}} \times \mathbf{L} - \mu k \frac{\mathbf{v}}{r} + \mu k \frac{r v}{r^2} \qquad [3.26]$$

since $\mathbf{L}$ is a constant. In the first term let us use $\dot{\mathbf{p}} = \mathbf{F} = -k\mathbf{r}/r^3$ and write $\mathbf{L} = \mu \mathbf{r} \times \mathbf{v}$. In the third term we use $\mathbf{r} \cdot \mathbf{v} = rv$ since they are both equal to $\frac{1}{2}d/dt(\mathbf{r} \cdot \mathbf{r}) = \frac{1}{2}d/dt(r^2)$, to express v as

$\mathbf{r} \cdot \mathbf{v}/r$ giving:

$$\dot{\mathbf{A}} = -\frac{\mu k}{r^3} \mathbf{r} \times (\mathbf{r} \times \mathbf{v}) - \frac{\mu k}{r} \mathbf{v} + \frac{\mu k}{r^3} (\mathbf{r} \cdot \mathbf{v})\mathbf{r}.$$

On expanding the triple product

$$\mathbf{r} \times (\mathbf{r} \times \mathbf{v}) = (\mathbf{r} \cdot \mathbf{v})\mathbf{r} - r^2 \mathbf{v} \qquad [3.27]$$

we obtain

$$\dot{\mathbf{A}} = -\frac{\mu k}{r^3} (\mathbf{r} \cdot \mathbf{v})\mathbf{r} + \frac{\mu k}{r} \mathbf{v} - \frac{\mu k}{r} \mathbf{v} + \frac{\mu k}{r^3} (\mathbf{r} \cdot \mathbf{v})\mathbf{r}.$$

The first term cancels the last and the second term cancels the third, so that

$$\dot{\mathbf{A}} = 0 \qquad [3.28]$$

and $\mathbf{A}$ is indeed a constant of the motion.

Of course there is no magic in this. The expression for $\mathbf{A}$ is chosen so that the time dependence of the second term cancels that of the first term for an inverse-square-law force. Furthermore, any combination of constants of the motion will also be a constant of the motion. The importance of the Runge–Lenz vector lies in the fact that the motion may be elegantly described in terms of it and that it has a simple useful interpretation, as we shall discover.

We note from the definition of $\mathbf{A}$ that it lies in the plane of motion, since as $\mathbf{L}$ is perpendicular to this plane $\mathbf{p} \times \mathbf{L}$ lies in the plane, as does $\mathbf{r}$.

The orbit may be found simply by taking the dot product of $\mathbf{A}$ with the position vector:

$$\mathbf{r} \cdot \mathbf{A} = \mathbf{r} \cdot \mathbf{p} \times \mathbf{L} - \mu k r.$$

We now write $\mathbf{r} \cdot \mathbf{A}$ as $rA \cos \phi$, where ϕ is the angle in the plane between the constant vector $\mathbf{A}$ and the position vector, as in Fig. 3.4. Also let us permute the scalar triple product

$$\mathbf{r} \cdot \mathbf{p} \times \mathbf{L} = \mathbf{r} \times \mathbf{p} \cdot \mathbf{L} = \mathbf{L} \cdot \mathbf{L} = L^2$$

so that we have

$$rA \cos \phi = L^2 - \mu k r$$

or

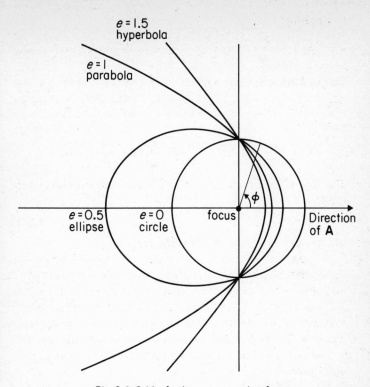

Fig. 3.4 Orbits for inverse-square-law force

$$\frac{1}{r} = \frac{\mu k}{L^2}\left(1 + \frac{A}{\mu k}\cos\phi\right) \qquad [3.29]$$

which is of course the polar equation for a conic section (ellipse, parabola, hyperbola) of eccentricity e, where

$$e = A/\mu k. \qquad [3.30]$$

We may relate A to the more familiar constants of the motion by substituting the above expression for the orbit into the differential equation for the orbit (equation [3.20]). After a little manipulation one finds

$$A^2 = \mu^2 k^2 + 2\mu E L^2 \qquad [3.31]$$

and in terms of this we may express the eccentricity of the orbit as

Dynamics of a single particle 45

$$e = \left(1 + \frac{2EL^2}{\mu k^2}\right)^{\frac{1}{2}}. \qquad\qquad [3.32]$$

The direction of **A** within the plane of motion may be found, recalling that ϕ is taken as the angle between **A** and the position vector **r**. So when $\cos \phi = 1$ or $\phi = 0$, **r** is parallel to **A**. From equation [3.29] we see that this makes **r** take its smallest value and so we conclude that **A** points to the position of closest approach or the *perihelion* of the orbit.

The magnitude and the sign of the energy determine the eccentricity of the motion, and according to the value of the eccentricity the orbit may be any of the conic sections:

$E > 0,$	$e > 1$	hyperbola
$E = 0,$	$e = 1$	parabola
$E < 0,$	$e < 1$	ellipse
$E = -\dfrac{\mu k^2}{2L^2},$	$e = 0$	circle.

This, then, extends the qualitative discussion in section 3.5. We see that the condition for circular orbit is the same as that derived from the equivalent one-dimensional problem (example 3.3).

3.7 Kepler's laws

Newton formulated his law of gravitation by saying that there is a force of mutual attraction between any two bodies of mass m_1 and m_2 whose strength is given by

$$F = -\frac{Gm_1m_2}{r^2}$$

where r is the distance separating them and G is a constant.

Recall that mass was introduced as the measure of inertia of a body, the constant of proportionality between the applied force and the resultant acceleration. This is a passive property—the body feels a force and moves accordingly. In contrast to this we now see another aspect of mass, an active one—with gravitation, mass now produces the force as well.

The equivalence of inertial mass and gravitational mass was

first demonstrated by Galileo when he dropped different weights off the leaning tower of Pisa (although he did not look at it in this way). Modern experiments have found no discernible difference, and Einstein was led to use this equivalence in the formulation of his general theory of relativity.

The potential energy function corresponding to the gravitational force is given by

$$V(r) = -\frac{Gm_1m_2}{r}$$

as may be verified by differentiation. In treating a planet of mass m orbiting the sun of mass M we have the same problem as treated in section 3.6 where we identify the constant k of equation [3.23] with

$$k = GmM. \tag{3.33}$$

But our present problem is a two-body problem. For example, it is the angular momentum of the sun–planet pair that is conserved. The reduction of the two-body problem to a one-body problem is treated in the next chapter in section 4.2. At this stage we simply note that for the two-body problem the mass μ of the previous section is to be taken as the harmonic mean of the two masses,

$$\mu = \frac{Mm}{M+m}$$

known as the *reduced mass*. However, when M is very much larger than m the difference between μ and the mass of the planet will be negligible.

In this section we shall recall Kepler's laws of planetary motion, discussed in section 1.1, to see if we can justify them from what we have established so far. We want to find out exactly how much physics is contained in the laws.

1. The path of a planet is an ellipse with the sun at one focus.

We established this in equation [3.29]. This result follows uniquely from an inverse-square-law force.

2. The line joining the planet to the sun sweeps out equal areas in equal times.

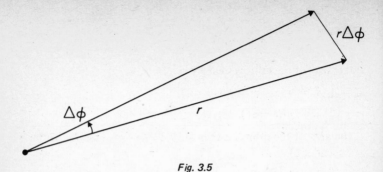

Fig. 3.5

This law is in fact simply a consequence of the conservation of angular momentum, and so it is true for any central force. We may see this by considering an element of the path swept out in time Δt (see Fig. 3.5). The area of the triangle ΔS is given by $\frac{1}{2}r^2\Delta\phi$, so the rate of change of area is found by dividing by Δt. In the limit of small Δt,

$$\frac{\mathrm{d}S}{\mathrm{d}t} = \frac{1}{2}r^2\frac{\mathrm{d}\phi}{\mathrm{d}t}.$$

But recalling the expression for angular momentum:

$$L = \mu r^2 \dot{\phi}$$

the rate of change of area is then given by

$$\frac{\mathrm{d}S}{\mathrm{d}t} = L/2\mu. \qquad [3.34]$$

So wherever angular momentum is conserved, equal areas are swept out in equal times.

   3. The square of the orbital period is proportional to the cube of the distance from the sun.

The simplest way to establish this law is from the area of the orbit. Then, using Kepler's second law, we can find the time it takes for one orbital revolution. However, we must first specify what we mean by the 'distance from the sun' for an elliptical orbit. We use the mean of the maximum and the minimum distance, which is equal to the size of the semi-major axis R.

   Using the polar equation for a conic

$$\frac{1}{r} = \frac{1}{\rho}(1 + e \cos \phi)$$

the 'size' of the orbit is then given by

$$R = \tfrac{1}{2}\{r(\phi=0) + r(\phi=\pi)\}$$
$$= \rho/(1-e^2).$$

The area of the orbit S is then given by (see exercise 7, chapter 3, Appendix 1)

$$S = \pi R^{3/2}\rho^{1/2}.$$

However we may relate the area of the orbit to the angular momentum L and the orbital period τ using equation [3.34]

$$S = \dot{S}\tau = L\tau/2\mu$$

so that

$$\pi R^{3/2}\rho^{1/2} = L\tau/2\mu.$$

By comparison with equation [3.29] we see that

$$\rho = \frac{L^2}{\mu k}$$

and thus we have

$$\tau^2 = (2\pi)^2 \frac{\mu}{k} R^3.$$

But the essence of Kepler's third law is that the proportionality of τ^2 to R^3 is the same for all planets. Since

$$k = GmM$$

and

$$\mu = \frac{mM}{m + M}$$

the 'constant' of proportionality is

$$\frac{\tau^2}{R^3} = \frac{(2\pi)^2}{G(m+M)}.$$ [3.35]

So this law is true when one can neglect the mass of the planet in comparison with the mass of the sun. The square of the period is proportional to the cube of the size of the orbit, the constant of proportionality depending on the mass of the sun and the gravitational constant G.

Example 3.4

The mean distance between the earth and the sun is observed to be 1.496×10^{11} m. Using Kepler's third law, find the mass of the sun.

Kepler's third law relates the distance to the orbital period. In this case the force constant k is GMm, where M is the mass of the sun and m the mass of the earth. The expression for the law is then (from equation [3.35])

$$\tau = \frac{2\pi R^{3/2}}{\sqrt{G(m + M)}}$$

Since the mass of the earth is so much less than that of the sun it may be ignored. The period of the earth's rotation is one year which is $365.25 \times 24 \times 60 \times 60 = 3.156 \times 10^7$ s, and the gravitational constant $G = 6.670 \times 10^{11}$ N m^2 kg^{-2}. The expression for the mass is

$$
\begin{aligned}
M &= \frac{4\pi^2 R^3}{G\tau^2} \\
&= \frac{4\pi^2 (1.496 \times 10^{11})^3}{6.670 \times 10^{-11} \times (3.156 \times 10^7)^2} \\
&= 1.99 \times 10^{30} \text{ kg.}
\end{aligned}
$$

This is in agreement with the accepted value.

Chapter 4
Many-particle systems

.1 Centre of mass

There is a sense in which a body made up of a number of parts (atoms, say) may be regarded as a point mass. We have made such an assumption in previous chapters, even when considering an object as large as the sun! It is the purpose of this section to investigate the extent to which this assumption is valid.

We shall consider a collection of point masses, the ith one having mass m_i and position $\mathbf{r}_i$. Now the rate of change of the momentum of the ith particle is equal to the force on that particle, and there are two contributions to this force. First, there is the externally applied force on this particle, $\mathbf{F}_i$, and, second, there is the internal force on the particle due to all the other particles, $\sum_j \mathbf{F}_{ij}$, where $\mathbf{F}_{ij}$ is the force on the ith particle from the jth particle. We can thus write

$$\dot{\mathbf{p}}_i = \mathbf{F}_i + \sum_j \mathbf{F}_{ij}.$$

Defining the total momentum $\mathbf{P}$ and the total externally applied force $\mathbf{F}$ by

$$\mathbf{P} = \sum_i \mathbf{p}_i \qquad\qquad [4.1]$$

$$\mathbf{F} = \sum_i \mathbf{F}_i \qquad\qquad [4.2]$$

we obtain the equation of motion for the total momentum:

$$\dot{\mathbf{P}} = \mathbf{F} + \sum_{ij} \mathbf{F}_{ij}.$$

Now, if the internal force obey Newton's third law, that is if

$$\mathbf{F}_{ij} = -\mathbf{F}_{ji}$$

then the sum of the internal forces vanishes and we are left with the equation of motion

$$\dot{\mathbf{p}} = \mathbf{F} \qquad [4.3]$$

i.e. the rate of change of total momentum is equal to the total externally applied force. We have thus recovered Newton's second law.

But in what sense may one regard this total momentum (equation [4.1]) as the momentum of a point mass? In other words, can we specify a mass and a position for this equivalent point mass? Mathematically, if we write

$$\mathbf{P} = M\dot{\mathbf{R}} \qquad [4.4]$$

what are M and $\mathbf{R}$? The total momentum is given by

$$\mathbf{P} = \frac{\mathrm{d}}{\mathrm{d}t} \sum_i m_i \mathbf{r}_i.$$

We have some sort of suspicion that the 'mass' M should be the total mass $\sum_i m_i$ of the assembly, so pulling out a factor of $\sum_i m_i$, the total momentum may be written as

$$\mathbf{P} = (\sum_i m_i) \frac{\mathrm{d}}{\mathrm{d}t} \frac{\sum_i m_i \mathbf{r}_i}{\sum_i m_i}.$$

This expression does have the desired form of equation [4.4] when we identify M as the total mass:

$$M = \sum_i m_i \qquad [4.5]$$

and $\mathbf{R}$ as the position of the equivalent point mass:

$$\mathbf{R} = \frac{\sum_i m_i \mathbf{r}_i}{\sum_i m_i}. \qquad [4.6]$$

We recognize $\mathbf{R}$ as the definition of the *centre of mass*. This may be regarded as the average position of the particles, each individual position $\mathbf{r}_i$ being weighted by its fractional mass m_i/M.

We see, then, that when an assembly of particles is acted on by an external force its centre of mass moves as if all the mass were concentrated at that point. In this sense, then, we can regard a macroscopic object as a point mass. An example of this is the trajectory of an exploding shell. The centre of mass of the fragments continues in the same trajectory as that before the disintegration (neglecting air friction).

Let us finally note that from equation [4.3] we see that in the absence of external force the total momentum of an assembly of particles remains constant — the centre of mass moves with a constant velocity.

4.2 The two-body problem

The simplest many-body problem is that of two bodies. As mentioned in section 3.7, the Kepler problem is in reality a two-body problem since the motion of the sun must be included. In this section we consider the motion of two particles interacting with a mutual force.

Let the particles have masses m_1 and m_2. Under the influence of a mutual force the equations of motion will be

$$m_1 \ddot{\mathbf{r}}_1 = \mathbf{F}_{12}$$
$$m_2 \ddot{\mathbf{r}}_2 = \mathbf{F}_{21}.$$

Assuming Newton's third law, we then obtain the equation of motion for the relative displacement $\mathbf{r}_{21} = \mathbf{r}_2 - \mathbf{r}_1$:

$$\ddot{\mathbf{r}}_{21} = \frac{\mathbf{F}_{21}}{m_2} - \frac{\mathbf{F}_{12}}{m_1}$$

$$= \mathbf{F}_{21} \left(\frac{1}{m_2} + \frac{1}{m_1} \right)$$

$$= \mathbf{F}_{21} \left(\frac{m_1 + m_2}{m_1 m_2} \right). \qquad [4.7]$$

Introducing the quantity μ where

$$\mu = \frac{m_1 m_2}{m_1 + m_2} \qquad [4.8]$$

we then have the equation of motion for the relative displacement:

$$\mu\ddot{\mathbf{r}}_{21} = \mathbf{F}_{21}. \qquad [4.9]$$

This is the same as an equation of motion for a single body of mass μ experiencing the force $\mathbf{F}_{21}$. The mass μ is termed the *reduced mass* of the system, and this then justifies the procedures adopted in chapter 3.

Incidentally, if one of the masses, say m_2, were infinite then the effective mass μ would be equal to m_1. Thus we may regard the introduction of the effective mass as the correction for the finite mass of the force centre.

What we have done in this and the last section is to separate the two-body problem into two one-body problems, i.e. the motion of the centre of mass and the motion of the relative coordinate. It must be emphasized that this complete separation is only possible for two bodies. In general all we can do is reduce an n-body problem to an $(n-1)$-body problem plus the one-body problem of the motion of the centre of mass. No further reduction is possible.

4.3 Energy of a many-particle system

We have seen that in the absence of external force the centre of mass moves with a constant velocity. It is then possible to perform a Galilean transformation to a frame in which the centre of mass is fixed. This will provide a simplification of the dynamical problem — separating the internal and external aspects of the system. In this section we shall see that the energy takes a particularly simple form when transformed in this way. We only need consider the kinetic energy, since the internal potential energy, depending on the inter-particle separation, will not be affected by a Galilean transformation.

In terms of the original coordinate $\mathbf{R}_i$ of the different particles, the kinetic energy is given by:

$$T = \tfrac{1}{2}\sum_i m_i \dot{\mathbf{R}}_i^2. \qquad [4.10]$$

We now introduce a new set of coordinates $\mathbf{r}_i$, measured in the frame of the centre of mass, $\mathbf{R}$:

$$\mathbf{R}_i = \mathbf{r}_i + \mathbf{R}.$$

The kinetic energy expressed in terms of the centre-of-mass coordinates is then given by

$$T = \tfrac{1}{2}\sum_i m_i(\dot{\mathbf{r}}_i + \dot{\mathbf{R}})^2 \qquad\qquad [4.11]$$

which may be multiplied out to give

$$T = \tfrac{1}{2}\sum_i m_i\dot{\mathbf{r}}_i^2 + \tfrac{1}{2}\sum_i m_i\dot{\mathbf{R}}^2 + \sum_i m_i\dot{\mathbf{r}}_i \cdot \dot{\mathbf{R}}. \qquad [4.12]$$

The third term vanishes as we shall now show. We take the expression $\sum_i m_i\mathbf{r}_i$ which we express in terms of the original coordinates:

$$\sum_i m_i\mathbf{r}_i = \sum_i m_i(\mathbf{R}_i - \mathbf{R})$$

$$= \sum_i m_i\mathbf{R}_i - M\mathbf{R}. \qquad\qquad [4.13]$$

However, recalling the definition of the centre of mass (equation [4.6])

$$\mathbf{R} = \sum_i m_i\mathbf{R}_i/M$$

we see that equation [4.13] is zero. We have, then, the result for the centre-of-mass coordinates:

$$\sum_i m_i\mathbf{r}_i = 0. \qquad\qquad [4.14]$$

Upon differentiation we find

$$\sum_i m_i\dot{\mathbf{r}}_i = 0 \qquad\qquad [4.15]$$

which causes the third term of equation [4.12] to vanish, as we sought to establish.

The kinetic energy expressed in terms of the centre-of-mass coordinates is then the sum of two terms:

$$T = \tfrac{1}{2}\sum_i m_i\dot{\mathbf{r}}_i^2 + \tfrac{1}{2}M\dot{\mathbf{R}}^2. \qquad\qquad [4.16]$$

The second term is the kinetic energy of the total mass moving with the centre of mass velocity, while the first term is the kinetic energy of the particles measured with respect to the centre of mass.

This separation allows us to neglect the overall motion of the system when considering the internal contribution to the energy. Since the potential energy remains unchanged, we can write for the total energy:

$$E_T = E_{CM} + \tfrac{1}{2}M\dot{\mathbf{R}}^2 \qquad [4.17]$$

where E_T is the total energy, E_{CM} is the energy measured in the centre-of-mass frame and the last term is the kinetic energy of the 'equivalent point mass'.

4.4 Angular momentum

In treating many-particle systems, a central role is played by Newton's third law. When we considered momentum and its conservation in a composite system the third law ensured that the internal forces had no influence on the centre of mass motion. In this section we shall see that the same is true for the total *angular* momentum.

The total angular momentum $\mathbf{L}$ is defined simply as the sum of the angular momenta of the component parts:

$$\mathbf{L} = \sum_i \mathbf{R}_i \times \mathbf{p}_i$$

$$= \sum_i m_i \mathbf{R}_i \times \dot{\mathbf{R}}_i. \qquad [4.18]$$

Our procedure is simply the many-body analogue of that for the angular momentum of a single particle (see section 2.5).

Differentiating $\mathbf{L}$ with respect to time we have

$$\dot{\mathbf{L}} = \sum_i m_i \mathbf{R}_i \times \ddot{\mathbf{R}}_i + \sum_i m_i \dot{\mathbf{R}}_i \times \dot{\mathbf{R}}_i.$$

But $\dot{\mathbf{R}}_i \times \dot{\mathbf{R}}_i = 0$ so the last term vanishes.

Now from Newton's second law

$$m_i \ddot{\mathbf{R}}_i = \mathbf{F}_i + \sum_j \mathbf{F}_{ij}$$

so that $\dot{\mathbf{L}}$ is given by

$$\dot{\mathbf{L}} = \sum_i \mathbf{R}_i \times \mathbf{F}_i + \sum_{ij} \mathbf{R}_i \times \mathbf{F}_{ij}.$$

In the second term we take the elements in the sum in pairs,

$$\mathbf{R}_i \times \mathbf{F}_{ij} + \mathbf{R}_j \times \mathbf{F}_{ji}.$$

Now by Newton's third law $\mathbf{F}_{ij} = -\mathbf{F}_{ji}$ so that the pair becomes

$$(\mathbf{R}_i - \mathbf{R}_j) \times \mathbf{F}_{ij}$$

and this is zero if the force $\mathbf{F}_{ij}$ is along the line joining the particle, $\mathbf{R}_i - \mathbf{R}_j$. These terms then all vanish and we are left with

$$\dot{\mathbf{L}} = \mathbf{N} \qquad\qquad [4.19]$$

where $\mathbf{N}$ is simply the total torque on the system:

$$\mathbf{N} = \sum_i \mathbf{R}_i \times \mathbf{F}_i. \qquad\qquad [4.20]$$

Thus the rate of change of total angular momentum is equal to the total torque. So the total angular momentum is conserved if the total externally applied torque is zero.

We shall now show that, in terms of the centre-of-mass coordinates, the expression for the angular momentum is simplified. Following the notation of section 4.3, if $\mathbf{r}_i$ is the position with respect to the centre of mass $\mathbf{R}$, the position of the ith particle $\mathbf{R}_i$ is

$$\mathbf{R}_i = \mathbf{r}_i + \mathbf{R}.$$

The total angular momentum may then be written as:

$$\mathbf{L} = \sum_i m_i(\mathbf{r}_i + \mathbf{R}) \times (\dot{\mathbf{r}}_i + \dot{\mathbf{R}})$$

$$= \sum m_i \mathbf{r}_i \times \dot{\mathbf{r}}_i - \dot{\mathbf{R}} \times \sum_i m_i \mathbf{r}_i + \mathbf{R} \times \sum_i m_i \dot{\mathbf{r}}_i + M\mathbf{R} \times \dot{\mathbf{R}}.$$

The second and third terms vanish, as established in equations [4.14] and [4.15], and we are then left with

$$\mathbf{L} = \sum_i m_i \mathbf{r}_i \times \dot{\mathbf{r}}_i + M\mathbf{R} \times \dot{\mathbf{R}} \qquad\qquad [4.21]$$

i.e. the total angular momentum may be expressed as the sum of the angular momentum of the constituents about the centre of mass, plus the angular momentum of the centre of mass.

4.5 Friction and dissipation

All macroscopic systems are subject to friction, the epitome of a non-conservative force. However, in origin friction is completely different from the other forces we have considered — electric, gravitational, elastic. The amplitude of a swinging pendulum decreases because of collisions between the air molecules and the bob. Although the interaction between the bob and each molecule may be conservative, the net result of a large number of collisions of random magnitude and direction is a loss of energy from the pendulum to the air.

In other words, although the many-body system of pendulum plus air molecules may be conservative, the same pendulum considered as a one-body problem is non-conservative. This is the nature of friction and dissipation in general. It is the result of a very large number of interactions which we do not care (or are not able) to treat exactly.

It will be recalled that friction is commonly treated as a negative force proportional to velocity. This is obviously non-conservative, as we have already seen in example 2.3. In this section we shall examine the microscopic explanation for friction and its velocity dependence.

We take as our model a large (on the atomic scale) mass travelling with a velocity V through a gas of moving atoms. As we shall restrict our attention to one dimension, vectors are not necessary. From exercise 2, chapter 2, Appendix 1, we find that a large mass M in collision with a small mass m with relative velocity v experiences a change in velocity of $2mv/M$. The change in velocity ΔV caused by collision with a small particle with velocity u is then given by

$$\Delta V = \frac{2m}{M}(u - V)$$

since $v = u - V$, and the change due to a collision with a particle moving in the opposite direction with the same speed is

$$\Delta V = \frac{2m}{M}(-u - V).$$

We shall add the effect of many collisions to find the mean change in velocity and hence the force. Since there will be on average equal numbers of atoms moving in either direction we shall start by adding these two contributions:

$$\Delta V = -\frac{2m}{M} V$$

giving a change in velocity independent of the speed of the atoms; we only need assume that the velocity distribution of the atoms is isotropic. Now assuming $2n$ such collisions per second, n from the left and n from the right, the mean change in velocity per unit time is given by

$$\frac{dV}{dt} = -2 \frac{m}{M} nV.$$

Since dV/dt is the acceleration, multiplying by the mass M of the body we obtain the equivalent force:

$$F = -2mnV. \qquad [4.22]$$

We have obtained a force proportional to velocity.

It must be emphasized that this is a simplified discussion of a special case. In general the force will not be exactly proportional to velocity, and in any case the retardation in reality occurs as a series of small jolts (Brownian motion). However, the broad features of this model may be taken over for other mechanisms of dissipation. The key element is that whereas collisions from the front impede motion and collisions from behind enhance it, the greater relative velocity of the front-ways collisions leads on average to a retardation of the motion.

Example 4.1

Show that, under the effect of friction, a falling body will reach a terminal velocity. Derive an expression describing how this velocity is reached.

The gravitational force is mg while the frictional force is $-\gamma v$, γ being the friction constant and v the velocity. The equation of motion is then

$$m\dot{v} = mg - \gamma v.$$

If there is a limiting velocity, then $\dot{v}$ will become zero, from which we find the terminal velocity $\dot{v}_t$:

$$0 = mg - \gamma v_t$$

or

$$v_t = \frac{mg}{\gamma}.$$

Let us now solve the equation of motion to see if this is the case. First we introduce a new variable s to remove the constant term from the equation:

$$s = v - \frac{mg}{\gamma}.$$

In terms of this, the equation of motion becomes

$$\dot{s} = v - \frac{\gamma}{m}s$$

and the solution is then

$$s(t) = s(0) \exp\left(-\frac{\gamma}{m}t\right)$$

or

$$v(t) = \frac{mg}{\gamma}\left\{1 - \exp\left(-\frac{\gamma}{m}t\right)\right\}$$

if the particle starts from zero velocity.

We see that the terminal velocity mg/γ is approached in an exponential manner, with a time constant m/γ.

4.6 Scattering

In principle the force field of a system may be studied by the use of a test particle. As this test object is moved from place to place the force at each point is noted. In this way one may build up a map of the whole force field. This idealization is not possible for microscopic objects, nor for systems whose interiors are inaccessible. For such cases the technique of *scattering* must be used. One shoots a stream of test particle — electrons, α particles, photons, etc. — at the system under investigation and one then observes the outcoming projectiles. In particular the extent to which the particles are deflected from their original path yields information about the forces they experience during their trajectory.

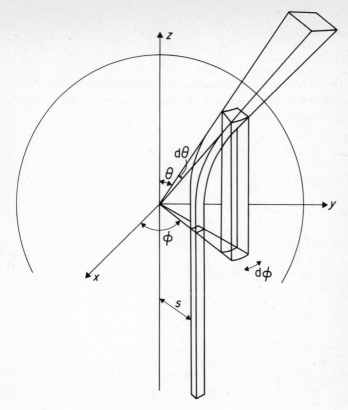

Fig. 4.1 Scattering of beam element $s \, ds \, d\phi$ by a central force

A single incident particle is specified in terms of its *impact parameter* s and its polar angle ϕ (see Fig. 4.1). The impact parameter (see Fig. 4.1) is defined as the perpendicular distance from the force centre to the initial path. A beam of particles will have a range of impact parameters and ϕ will range from 0 to 2π. The outgoing particles will then be scattered through a corresponding range of angles.

The *intensity* I of the incoming beam is given by the number of particles crossing unit area perpendicular to the beam in unit time. Let us now consider an element of the beam with impact parameter between s and $s + ds$, and polar angle between ϕ and $\phi + d\phi$. The perpendicular area of this element is $s\,ds\,d\phi$, and the number of particles dn crossing this per second is then $Is\,ds\,d\phi$:

$$dn = Is\,ds\,d\phi. \qquad [4.23]$$

These will be scattered through an angle of between θ and $\theta + d\theta$, where θ is a function of s. We shall restrict our consideration to central forces so that the scattered beam also has a polar angle of between ϕ and $\phi + d\phi$, and the scattering angle is independent of ϕ.

The area of a unit sphere that the scattered beam will cover is given by $\sin\theta\,d\theta\,d\phi$, so that the scattered intensity I_s is given by

$$I_s = \frac{dn}{\sin\theta\,d\theta\,d\phi}$$

or, using equation [4.23],

$$\frac{I_s}{I} = \frac{s\,ds}{\sin\theta\,d\theta}.$$

This ratio is known as the *differential scattering cross-section* and is denoted by σ:

$$\sigma(\theta) = \frac{s}{\sin\theta}\left|\frac{ds}{d\theta}\right| \qquad [4.24]$$

where we have taken the magnitude of $ds/d\theta$ since the number of particles must be positive even if s and θ vary in opposite directions.

It is this quantity $\sigma(\theta)$ that is measured in practice. A particle detector on a swinging arm is moved around, changing θ, and the particle count at each position recorded.

The principal task, then, in the theory of scattering is to relate scattering angle as a function of impact parameter, $\theta(s)$, to the force law or the corresponding potential energy function $V(r)$. This may be done in the general case by solving the integral for the path (equation [3.21]). Once the path is known, the scattering angle may easily be found as the following example demonstrates.

Example 4.2

A particle is scattered from an inverse-square-law force. Calculate the angle of scattering. Express this angle (1) in terms of the eccentricity of the hyperbolic path and (2) in terms of the energy and impact parameter.

We know that the shape of the trajectory is a hyperbola:

$$\frac{1}{r} = \frac{1}{\rho}(1 + e \cos \phi)$$

where $e > 1$ is the eccentricity. The orientation of the incoming and outgoing asymptotes to the path is the values of ϕ for which $r \to \infty$ or $1/r \to 0$. That is

$$1 + e \cos \phi = 0$$

or

$$\cos \phi = -\frac{1}{e}.$$

From Fig. 4.2 we see that

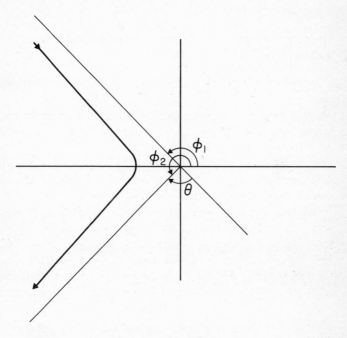

Fig. 4.2 Angles in scattering problem

$$\sin \frac{\theta}{2} = -\cos \phi = \frac{1}{e}$$

thus

$$\sin \frac{\theta}{2} = \frac{1}{e}.$$

Now, relating this to the impact parameter and the energy, we have the expression for the eccentricity (equation [3.32]):

$$e = \left(1 + \frac{2EL^2}{\mu k^2}\right)^{\frac{1}{2}}.$$

Since

$$E = \tfrac{1}{2}\mu v_0^2$$

and

$$L = \mu v_0 s$$

where v_0 is the initial velocity, we obtain

$$L = s(2\mu E)^{\frac{1}{2}}$$

so that

$$e = \left(1 + \frac{4E^2 s^2}{k^2}\right)^{\frac{1}{2}} = \operatorname{cosec} \theta/2 \qquad [4.25]$$

since $\sin \theta/2 = 1/e$. Squaring this:

$$1 + \frac{4E^2 s^2}{k^2} = \operatorname{cosec}^2 \theta/2 = 1 + \cot^2 \theta/2$$

which gives

$$\cot \frac{\theta}{2} = \frac{2Es}{k}. \qquad [4.26]$$

This is the required relation for the scattering angle.

4.7 Rutherford scattering

Rutherford used a beam of alpha particles to study the structure of atoms. Up to that time the popular view of the atom was embodied in Thomson's 'plum pudding' model. According to this there was a positive charge spread over the volume of the atom (the pudding) and sufficient negatively charged electrons dotted around (the plums) to produce an atom with no overall electrical charge.

The alpha particle consists of two protons and two neutrons, i.e. a helium nucleus. Its positive charge makes it sensitive to the electric fields inside the atom and hence the internal charge distribution.

According to Thomson's model one would not expect the alpha particles incident on a thin foil to be deflected significantly. To Rutherford's surprise, however, there was considerable scattering. Some alpha particles were even reflected, i.e. scattered through 180°! In his own words 'it was as if you had fired a 15" shell at a sheet of tissue paper and it came back and hit you'. He realized that the positive charge of the atom had to be concentrated at its centre, and this suggested that the electrons orbited around it like a miniature solar system. To calculate the scattering cross-section due to the Coulomb interaction he exploited the analogy with the gravitational interaction and took over old-established results from his undergraduate text-books.

Denoting the charge on the proton by Q, the charge of an alpha particle is then $2Q$. The charge of the nucleus of an atom of atomic number Z is ZQ, so the force between the nucleus and an alpha particle, given by Coulomb's law, is:

$$F = \frac{2ZQ^2}{4\pi\epsilon_0 r^2}$$
$$= \frac{ZQ^2}{2\pi\epsilon_0 r^2}.$$

We relate this to our previous results by identifying the force constant k of chapter 3 (equation [3.23]) with the atomic properties:

$$k = -\frac{ZQ^2}{2\pi\epsilon_0} \qquad [4.27]$$

the minus sign indicating a repulsive rather than an attractive force.

One then takes over directly the result from section 4.6 for the inverse-square-law force (equation [4.26]):

$$\cot \frac{\theta}{2} = \frac{2Es}{k}.$$

The differential scattering cross-section is given by equation [4.24]:

$$\sigma(\theta) = \frac{s}{\sin \theta} \left| \frac{\mathrm{d}s}{\mathrm{d}\theta} \right|$$

so differentiating equation [4.26] we obtain:

$$\frac{\mathrm{d}s}{\mathrm{d}\theta} = \frac{k}{4E} \cot \frac{\theta}{2}$$

and

$$\sigma(\theta) = \frac{k^2}{16E^2} \operatorname{cosec}^4 \frac{\theta}{4}.$$

Substituting for k from equation [4.27] we then obtain Rutherford's famous formula:

$$\sigma(\theta) = \left(\frac{ZQ^2}{8E\pi\epsilon_0} \right)^2 \operatorname{cosec}^4 \theta/2. \qquad [4.28]$$

The experimental results are in close agreement with this formula, confirming Rutherford's model. He was rather lucky that this formula, derived classically, holds for quantum mechanics (non-relativistic). Although in quantum theory one cannot calculate the precise trajectory of a particle, one can talk of the observed particle flux, and that is what is measured. Fortunately, the quantum and classical calculations of the flux give identical results. Rutherford was also lucky that he did not examine his planetary model in greater detail, since classically accelerating charges (electrons in orbits) should radiate electromagnetic energy and spiral into the nucleus! It is only in quantum mechanics that charges can seem to accelerate without radiating.

4.8 Rockets and variable-mass systems

Caution must be exercised in applying Newton's laws to systems of variable mass. In this respect the restatement of Newton's second law $m\ddot{\mathbf{r}} = \mathbf{F}$ in the form $\dot{\mathbf{p}} = \mathbf{F}$ is not only misleading, it is in fact downright wrong. Since momentum is given by $\mathbf{p} = m\dot{\mathbf{r}}$, one might be induced to write the generalization of Newton's second law as

$$m\ddot{\mathbf{r}} + \dot{m}\dot{\mathbf{r}} = \mathbf{F} \text{ (false)}. \qquad [4.29]$$

This equation is wrong. If one *is* going to use the concept of momentum (rather than the straightforward use of $m\ddot{\mathbf{r}} = \mathbf{F}$), then the momentum of the lost or gained mass must be considered as well.

We shall consider the motion of a rocket as a typical example of a variable-mass system, and we shall look at it from the point of view of momentum. The momentum of a rocket *plus* the momentum of the exhaust is a conserved quantity. The centre of mass does not accelerate. It is the emission of the exhaust which causes the rocket to accelerate.

Let us take a rocket of mass M moving with a velocity V in a given inertial frame (see Fig. 4.3). At time interval $\mathrm{d}t$ later the rocket mass will have become $M + \mathrm{d}M$ (although $\mathrm{d}M$ will be negative in this case), and the velocity will have become $V + \mathrm{d}V$. The velocity of the exhaust relative to the rocket will be denoted by v, so that in our inertial frame it will be $v - V$ away from the rocket. In the time $\mathrm{d}t$ the mass of the exhaust emitted will be $-\mathrm{d}M$.

We may then write the total momentum as

$$\text{time } t \quad p = MV$$
$$\text{time } t + \mathrm{d}t \quad p = (M + \mathrm{d}M)(V + \mathrm{d}V) - \mathrm{d}M\,(V - v).$$

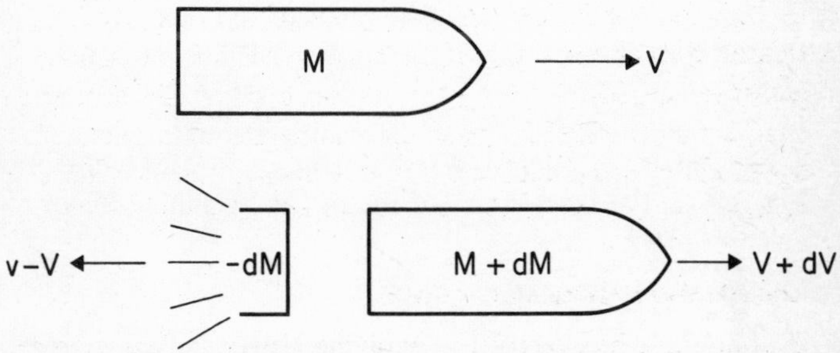

Fig. 4.3 Rocket change of mass in time dt

Equating these expressions we obtain

$$M \, dV + v \, dM = 0 \qquad [4.30]$$

or

$$dV = -v \, d \ln M.$$

Assuming the exhaust velocity v is constant, we may integrate this equation to give

$$V = V_0 + v \ln M/M_0 \qquad [4.31]$$

where V_0 and M_0 are the velocity and mass of the rocket at some given time.

If we take V_0, the initial velocity of the rocket, to be zero and M_0 to be the initial mass, we see that the final velocity of the rocket depends on the mass ratio and the exhaust velocity, regardless of the rate the exhaust is emitted.

Let us now consider the force on the rocket and its equation of motion. Dividing equation [4.30] by dt we obtain

$$M \frac{dV}{dt} + v \frac{dM}{dt} = 0. \qquad [4.32]$$

Denoting the rate at which the exhaust mass leaves the rocket by α,

$$\alpha = -\frac{dM}{dt} \qquad [4.33]$$

the equation of motion is then

$$M \frac{dV}{dt} = \alpha v.$$

The force on the rocket, or *thrust* as it is called, is given by

$$F = \alpha v. \qquad [4.34]$$

As a matter of interest, we may write the equation of motion in terms of the momentum of the rocket by adding $V dM/dt$ to equation [4.32], giving:

$$\frac{d}{dt}(MV) + v \frac{dM}{dt} = V \frac{dM}{dt}$$

or
$$\dot{\mathbf{p}} = (V-v)\dot{M}.$$

We see that the momentum of the rocket alone is not a very useful parameter.

Chapter 5
Rigid bodies and non-inertial frames

5.1 Rigid bodies

We are now dealing with a special case of a many-particle system, albeit an idealization. A rigid body is understood as an assembly of particles interacting with forces that are so 'stiff' that the separation between any two particles remains constant. From the considerations of the previous chapter we know that these internal forces do not affect the dynamics of the body. What distinguishes a rigid body from a point mass is its extension in space. This means that it must be described by its *orientation* as well as its location, i.e. six variables rather than three. Our task in the following sections must be to identify suitable variables to use, and to set up equations of motion for them in order to describe the change of these variables.

Change of location is simply translational motion. We have already seen that translation of a body (rigid or otherwise) may be treated simply as translation of an equivalent point object, the centre of mass. In other words there is no interesting new physics in the translational motion of rigid bodies. Thus we come to rotation, i.e. change of orientation.

It is obvious that the most general motion of a rigid body is a combination of translation and rotation. Furthermore, the axis of rotation may be chosen to pass through any point. This has been formalized into what is known as Euler's theorem of rigid-body motion. Now this has an important consequence, since in chapter 4 we saw that the energy and the angular momentum of a many-particle system could be expressed as the sum of the

contributions from the motion *of* the centre of mass and the
contribution of the motion *about* the centre of mass. By virtue of
Euler's theorem we may choose the axis of rotation to pass
through the centre of mass, resulting in complete separation of
translational and rotational motion. The interesting new physics
comes from a consideration of the rotational part of the motion.

We must commence, then, with an examination of the way
vectors behave under rotation.

.2 Rotating vectors

If we consider a vector fixed in a rotating body, the vector will
appear to change as the body is observed to rotate. In this section
we shall see how the observed rate of change of such a vector is
related to the rotation of the body.

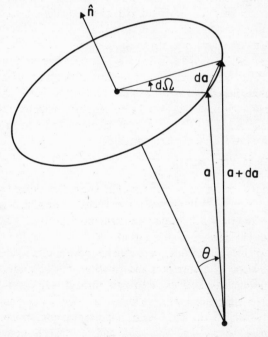

Fig. 5.1 Effect of rotation of a vector a through an angle dΩ

We start by considering a vector **a** which is constant in a frame rotating about an axis $\hat{n}$, and we calculate its increment d**a** under an infinitesimal rotation (see Fig. 5.1).

The direction of d**a** is perpendicular to the vector **a** and perpendicular to the axis of rotation $\hat{n}$, so it must be parallel to their vector cross product,

$$\text{d}\mathbf{a} \parallel \hat{n} \times \mathbf{a}.$$

The length of the vector d**a** is given by the product of the infinitesimal angle $\text{d}\Omega$ and the radius of the circle swept out, $a \sin \theta$. Thus:

$$|\text{d}\mathbf{a}| = \text{d}\Omega \, a \sin \theta.$$

Now the expressions for the magnitude and direction of d**a** may be combined by introducing an infinitesimal rotation vector $\text{d}\boldsymbol{\Omega}$ whose magnitude is the infinitesimal angle $\text{d}\Omega$ and whose direction is the axis of rotation $\hat{n}$:

$$\text{d}\boldsymbol{\Omega} = \text{d}\Omega \hat{n}.$$

We may then write for the direction of d**a**

$$\text{d}\mathbf{a} \parallel \text{d}\boldsymbol{\Omega} \times \mathbf{a}$$

and for the magnitude

$$|\text{d}\mathbf{a}| = |\text{d}\boldsymbol{\Omega} \times \mathbf{a}|.$$

In other words

$$\text{d}\mathbf{a} = \text{d}\boldsymbol{\Omega} \times \mathbf{a}$$

the increment of the vector **a** due to the incremental rotation $\text{d}\boldsymbol{\Omega}$.

If these increments occur in a time $\text{d}t$, then we may divide by $\text{d}t$ to obtain

$$\frac{\text{d}\mathbf{a}}{\text{d}t} = \frac{\text{d}\boldsymbol{\Omega}}{\text{d}t} \times \mathbf{a}$$

or, in terms of the angular velocity

$$\boldsymbol{\omega} = \frac{\text{d}\boldsymbol{\Omega}}{\text{d}t},$$

we have

$$\frac{d\mathbf{a}}{dt} = \boldsymbol{\omega} \times \mathbf{a}. \qquad [5.1]$$

This result was derived for the case where $\mathbf{a}$ has no implicit time dependence. If $\mathbf{a}$ is varying in the rotating frame and we denote its time derivative, measured in the rotating frame, by $\partial\mathbf{a}/\partial t$, then the time derivative as seen from the non-rotating frame is given by

$$\frac{d\mathbf{a}}{dt} = \boldsymbol{\omega} \times \mathbf{a} + \frac{\partial\mathbf{a}}{\partial t}. \qquad [5.2]$$

This result will be used frequently in the following section.

5.3   The inertia tensor

In this section we shall obtain expressions for the kinetic energy and the angular momentum of a rigid body in rotation. We shall see that the mass distribution of the body will be specified in terms of its *inertia tensor*.

Let us regard a rigid body as an assembly of point masses located at positions $\mathbf{r}$, as measured in a frame fixed in the body (in this section we reserve subscripts for vector components). In this frame the $\mathbf{r}$ are constant, so if the body is rotating with angular velocity $\boldsymbol{\omega}$ the velocity of a particle will be, by equation [5.2],

$$\dot{\mathbf{r}} = \boldsymbol{\omega} \times \mathbf{r}$$

and its angular momentum will then be

$$\begin{aligned} \mathbf{l} &= m\mathbf{r} \times \dot{\mathbf{r}} \\ &= m\mathbf{r} \times (\boldsymbol{\omega} \times \mathbf{r}). \qquad [5.3] \end{aligned}$$

Expanding the vector triple product and summing over all particles we obtain the total angular momentum:

$$\mathbf{L} = \sum_{\text{particles}} m\{\boldsymbol{\omega}\mathbf{r}^2 - \mathbf{r}(\mathbf{r} \cdot \boldsymbol{\omega})\}. \qquad [5.4]$$

Each component of $\mathbf{L}$ is seen to depend linearly on the components of $\boldsymbol{\omega}$. In other words we may regard this expression as a matrix product

$$\mathbf{L} = \mathbf{I}\boldsymbol{\omega}$$

which in terms of a set of components x, y, z would be

$$L_i = \sum_{j=x,y,z} I_{ij}\omega_j.$$

The object represented by $\mathbf{I}$, components I_{ij}, is known as the *inertia tensor*. Multiplying out equation [5.4] we obtain

$$I_{ij} = \sum_{\substack{\text{particles}}} m(\mathbf{r}^2\delta_{ij} - r_i r_j) \qquad [5.5]$$

or, in component form,

$$\mathbf{I} \sim \begin{bmatrix} \Sigma m(y^2 + z^2) & -\Sigma mxy & -\Sigma mxz \\ -\Sigma myx & \Sigma m(x^2 + z^2) & -\Sigma myz \\ -\Sigma mzx & -\Sigma mzy & \Sigma m(x^2 + y^2) \end{bmatrix}$$

$$[5.6]$$

We note that the diagonal elements of the inertia tensor are the moments of inertia about the corresponding axis. Furthermore, $\mathbf{I}$ is seen to be a symmetric tensor:

$$I_{ij} = I_{ji}.$$

The kinetic energy of a rigid body may also be expressed in terms of the inertia tensor. We have already found the velocity of a constituent particle of the body:

$$\dot{\mathbf{r}} = \boldsymbol{\omega} \times \mathbf{r}$$

so that the kinetic energy of the particle is then given by

$$T = \frac{m}{2}\dot{\mathbf{r}} \cdot \dot{\mathbf{r}}$$

$$= \frac{m}{2}(\boldsymbol{\omega} \times \mathbf{r}) \cdot (\boldsymbol{\omega} \times \mathbf{r}).$$

We permute this as a triple product and sum over all the particles in the body. The total kinetic energy is then given by

$$T = \tfrac{1}{2} \sum_{\substack{\text{particles}}} m\,\boldsymbol{\omega} \cdot \{\mathbf{r} \times (\boldsymbol{\omega} \times \mathbf{r})\}$$

$$= \tfrac{1}{2}\boldsymbol{\omega} \cdot \sum_{\substack{\text{particles}}} m\{\mathbf{r} \times (\boldsymbol{\omega} \times \mathbf{r})\}$$

from which we can identify the angular momentum as in equation [5.3]. The kinetic energy may then be expressed as

$$T = \tfrac{1}{2}\boldsymbol{\omega} \cdot \mathbf{L} \qquad\qquad [5.7]$$

or, in tensor form, since $\mathbf{L} = \mathsf{I}\boldsymbol{\omega}$,

$$T = \tfrac{1}{2}\boldsymbol{\omega}^{\mathrm{T}} \mathsf{I}\boldsymbol{\omega}. \qquad\qquad [5.8]$$

$\boldsymbol{\omega}^{\mathrm{T}}$ is the transpose of the vector $\boldsymbol{\omega}$, i.e. it is the row vector whose components are the same as those of the column vector $\boldsymbol{\omega}$.

If we regard the mass of a body as being continuously distributed according to a density function $\rho(\mathbf{r})$, then by analogy with equation [5.5] the inertia tensor would be given by an integral over the volume:

$$I_{ij} = \int\limits_{\text{volume}} \rho(\mathbf{r})\{\mathbf{r}^2\delta_{ij} - r_i r_j\}\,\mathrm{d}V. \qquad\qquad [5.9]$$

We have seen that the inertia tensor—or, to be precise, the matrix representing it—is always symmetric. In such cases it is always possible to find a set of coordinate axes in terms of which the matrix is diagonal. Such axes are known as the *principal axes* of the body and clearly they will be related to any axes of symmetry the body might have. The corresponding diagonal elements, the eigenvalues of the inertia tensor, are known as the *principal moments of inertia*.

In conclusion, this section has suggested that the inertia tensor of a rigid body is the intrinsic property of importance for consideration of its dynamics, supplementing mass, which is all that is necessary when considering a point object. In the next section we shall use the results of this section to derive the equations of motion for a rigid body.

5.4 The Euler equations for rigid-body motion

The rotation of a body is governed by the rotational analogue of Newton's second law (equation [2.23]), as generalized to many-particle systems in section 4.4: the rate of change of total angular momentum is equal to the applied torque

$$\frac{d\mathbf{L}}{dt} = \mathbf{N}$$

where the derivative must be evaluated in an inertial frame.

Denoting the derivative in the rotating frame by $\partial/\partial t$, we then have

$$\frac{d\mathbf{L}}{dt} = \frac{\partial\mathbf{L}}{\partial t} + \boldsymbol{\omega} \times \mathbf{L} \qquad [5.10]$$

so that the equation of motion in the body frame is

$$\frac{\partial\mathbf{L}}{\partial t} + \boldsymbol{\omega} \times \mathbf{L} = \mathbf{N}$$

or

$$\frac{\partial\mathbf{L}}{\partial t} = -\boldsymbol{\omega} \times \mathbf{L} + \mathbf{N} \qquad [5.11]$$

where $-\boldsymbol{\omega} \times \mathbf{L}$ now appears as a fictitious (centrifugal) torque arising because of the non-inertial nature of the body frame.

A considerable simplification of these equations occurs if one uses a coordinate system based on the principal axes, since then

$$\left.\begin{aligned} L_1 &= I_1\omega_1 \\ L_2 &= I_2\omega_2 \\ L_3 &= I_3\omega_3 \end{aligned}\right\} \qquad [5.12]$$

where I_1, I_2, I_3 are the principal moments of inertia. In terms of these, the equations of motion (equation [5.11]) become

$$\left.\begin{aligned} I_1\dot{\omega}_1 &= \omega_2\omega_3(I_2 - I_3) + N_1 \\ I_2\dot{\omega}_2 &= \omega_3\omega_1(I_3 - I_1) + N_2 \\ I_3\dot{\omega}_3 &= \omega_1\omega_2(I_1 - I_2) + N_3 \, . \end{aligned}\right\} \qquad [5.13]$$

These are the *Euler equations* for rigid-body motion.

Two points should be noted. First, these are non-linear equations and are therefore difficult to solve in the general case. Second, one must remember that the axes 1, 2, 3 (the principal axes) are fixed in the body, so any externally applied force must be resolved along axes moving with the body.

Example 5.1 The spherical top

This is the name given to a body whose three principal moments of inertia are equal, i.e. $I_1 = I_2 = I_3 = I$. Solve the equations of motion for a general torque.

The Euler equations in this case reduce to

$$\dot{\omega}_1 = N_1/I$$
$$\dot{\omega}_2 = N_2/I$$
$$\dot{\omega}_3 = N_3/I$$

or

$$\dot{\boldsymbol{\omega}} = \mathbf{N}/I.$$

Assuming N depends on time, we may integrate this equation to obtain the solution

$$\boldsymbol{\omega}(t) = \int^t \mathbf{N}(\tau)\mathrm{d}\tau/I.$$

In the case of zero torque we see that the angular velocity remains constant.

The Euler equations in the absence of torque reduce to

$$\left.\begin{aligned} I_1\dot{\omega}_1 &= \omega_2\omega_3(I_2 - I_3) \\ I_2\dot{\omega}_2 &= \omega_3\omega_1(I_3 - I_1) \\ I_3\dot{\omega}_3 &= \omega_1\omega_2(I_1 - I_2) \end{aligned}\right\} \qquad [5.14]$$

and these equations can (with difficulty) be solved in terms of elliptical integrals. The solution may then be written in terms of the constants of the motion, angular momentum and kinetic energy. Rather than do this, we shall simply consider some illuminating special cases in the following sections.

Except in the case of the spherical top, the angular momentum is not proportional and parallel to the angular velocity. This means that even though the angular momentum may be a constant of the motion, the angular velocity will not. In general the angular velocity vector will move around the angular momentum vector—known as *precession*—and the angle between these two vectors will vary—known as *nutation*.

5.5 The symmetrical top

The spherical top was trivial. The problem of motion of a general body is complex. An intermediate case, the symmetrical top, is fairly straightforward and serves to illuminate some of the interesting physics in the non-trivial cases.

The symmetrical top is defined as having two principal moments of inertia equal—imagine a body of cylindrical symmetry—it may even look like a top!

Let us take $I_1 = I_2 = I$. Then the Euler equations, in the absence of torque, become

$$\left. \begin{array}{l} I\,\dot{\omega}_1 = \omega_2\omega_3(I - I_3) \\ I\,\dot{\omega}_2 = \omega_3\omega_1(I_3 - I) \\ I_3\dot{\omega}_3 = 0. \end{array} \right\} \qquad [5.15]$$

The last equation tells us that ω_3 is a constant.

Defining a new constant α by

$$\alpha = \omega_3\left(\frac{I_3 - I}{I_1}\right)$$

the equations for ω_1 and ω_2 become

$$\left. \begin{array}{l} \dot{\omega}_1 = -\alpha\omega_2 \\ \dot{\omega}_2 = \alpha\omega_1. \end{array} \right\} \qquad [5.16]$$

These are solved by differentiating the first and substituting the second:

$$\ddot{\omega}_1 = -\alpha^2\omega_1.$$

On integrating we then obtain

$$\omega_1(t) = A\cos\alpha t$$

and similarly

$$\omega_2(t) = A\sin\alpha t.$$

The projection of the angular velocity vector in the $1, 2$ plane (the plane of symmetry) sweeps out a circle with angular frequency α. The length of its projection in this plane is constant, as is its projection on the 3-axis. Thus the length of the vector is constant and we may write the complete solution as

$$\omega_1(t) = \omega \sin \beta \cos \alpha t$$
$$\omega_2(t) = \omega \sin \beta \sin \alpha t \qquad [5.17]$$
$$\omega_3(t) = \omega \cos \beta$$

where β is the angle between the vector ω and the 3-axis (see Fig. 5.2).

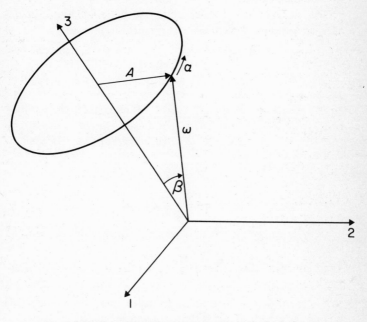

Fig. 5.2 Motion of angular velocity vector in the body frame

We see that the axis of rotation moves around the axis of symmetry with an angular frequency α. Of course this motion is occurring with respect to the body axes and these are rotating in space with angular velocity ω. So, viewed from a non-rotating frame, one observes the rotation at rate α superimposed on the rotation at rate ω.

5.6 Stability of rotational motion

Although we shall not treat the general motion of an asymmetrical body, the case of rotation about a principal axis is of importance, and simple to solve—rotation at constant angular velocity. In this section we examine the equation of the stability of rotation about the principal axes. There are important practical applications here, ranging from the stability of spinning satellites to the nature of the motion of a person falling down a mountainside.

We shall see that stable rotation occurs about the principal axes of the greatest and the least moment of inertia, while about the median axis the rotation is unstable. Try this by throwing a block of wood in the air spinning about its various axes.

We consider a body rotating about one of its principal axes, say 1, and we examine the effect of a perturbation producing a small rotation about the other axes. Let us examine the resultant small motion about the 2-axis. This is best treated by calculating the second derivative of ω_2. Differentiating the second of equations [5.14] we obtain

$$I_2\ddot{\omega}_2 = (\dot{\omega}_3\omega_1 + \omega_3\dot{\omega}_1)(I_3 - I_1).$$

Substituting for $\dot{\omega}_1$ and $\dot{\omega}_3$:

$$I_2\ddot{\omega}_2 = \omega_1^2\omega_2\frac{(I_1 - I_2)}{I_3} + \omega_2\omega_3^2\frac{(I_2 - I_3)(I_3 - I_1)}{I_1}. \quad [5.18]$$

Now the main motion is about axis 1, so that ω_2 and ω_3 are regarded as being very small while ω_1 is essentially constant. The first term with $\omega_1^2\omega_2$ is thus first order in smallness while the second term with $\omega_2\omega_3^2$ is third order in smallness, and may thus be neglected. The approximate equation of motion for ω_2 then has the form

$$\ddot{\omega}_2 = \lambda\omega_2$$

where

$$\lambda = \omega_1^2\frac{(I_1 - I_2)(I_3 - I_1)}{I_3 I_2}$$

The behaviour of ω_2 depends crucially on the sign of λ. For negative λ, ω_2 will execute simple harmonic motion of constant amplitude while positive λ implies exponential growth of ω_2, i.e. it is clearly unstable. The condition for stable motion may then be written as

$$(I_1 - I_2)(I_3 - I_1) < 0.$$

This is equivalent to

$$I_1 < I_2 \quad \text{and} \quad I_1 < I_3$$

or

$$I_1 > I_2 \quad \text{and} \quad I_1 > I_3. \qquad [5.19]$$

The motion is seen to be stable if rotation is about the principal axis of greatest or least principal moment of inertia.

In the presence of friction, only rotation about the axis of greatest principal moment of inertia is stable. A person falling off a mountain always ends up falling head over heels. However, the analysis of the dissipative case is too complex to consider here.

The advent of spacecraft has rekindled interest in these stability problems, and many of the old-established results are now being rediscovered.

5.7 Particle in a rotating frame

We now turn our attention to another aspect of rotating systems, the motion of a particle in a rotating frame of reference. In other words we shall observe the motion of an object through the eyes of someone in a rotating frame.

In an inertial frame, Newton's second law takes its familiar form:

$$m \frac{d^2\mathbf{r}}{dt^2} = \mathbf{F}. \qquad [5.20]$$

To evaluate $d^2\mathbf{r}/dt^2$ in terms of the variables of the rotating frame we use the transformation expression in equation [5.2]:

$$\frac{d\mathbf{a}}{dt} = \frac{\partial \mathbf{a}}{\partial t} + \boldsymbol{\omega} \times \mathbf{a}$$

so that

$$\frac{d^2\mathbf{r}}{dt^2} = \frac{\partial}{\partial t} + \boldsymbol{\omega} \times \frac{\partial \mathbf{r}}{\partial t} + \boldsymbol{\omega} \times \mathbf{r}$$

$$= \frac{\partial^2 \mathbf{r}}{\partial t^2} + 2\boldsymbol{\omega} \times \frac{\partial \mathbf{r}}{\partial t} + \boldsymbol{\omega} \times (\boldsymbol{\omega} \times \mathbf{r}) \qquad [5.21]$$

where we have assumed that the rotation is at constant angular velocity.

The equation of motion obtained from equation [5.20] then takes the form

$$m\ddot{\mathbf{r}} + 2m\boldsymbol{\omega} \times \dot{\mathbf{r}} + m\boldsymbol{\omega} \times (\boldsymbol{\omega} \times \mathbf{r}) = \mathbf{F} \qquad [5.22]$$

where we use a dot to denote differentiation in the rotating frame.

We may re-write this equation as

$$m\ddot{\mathbf{r}} = \mathbf{F}'$$

which is telling us that in the rotating frame an observer (who believes in Newton's laws) attributes his acceleration $\ddot{\mathbf{r}}$ to a force $\mathbf{F}'$, which we call an *effective* force. It is made up of the real force $\mathbf{F}$ and a *fictitious* force

$$-2m\boldsymbol{\omega} \times \dot{\mathbf{r}} - m\boldsymbol{\omega} \times (\boldsymbol{\omega} \times \mathbf{r})$$

due to the rotation.

The first term is a force that depends on the velocity in the rotating frame. The force is in the plane of rotation, at right angles to the motion of the particle. It is called the *Coriolis* force. A stationary particle does not experience a Coriolis force.

The second term does not depend on the velocity. The force is again in the plane of rotation and it is directed outward from the centre of rotation. It is known as the *centrifugal* force.

The Coriolis force due to the rotation of the earth has an important effect on the atmospheric winds. Whereas one would expect air to flow from regions of high pressure to regions of low pressure, perpendicular to the isobars, in fact the Coriolis force causes the winds to blow along the isobars. In the northern hemisphere winds travel anticlockwise around regions of low pressure while in the southern hemisphere they travel clockwise. Another example of the Coriolis force is the flow of the Gulf Stream, and of course there is the practical demonstration of the

Foucault pendulum. It is a matter of contention whether the flow of water down the plug-hole of a bath is due to the Coriolis force or not!

Fictitious forces always arise when one is in a non-inertial frame. If we relate the coordinates of a point measured in an inertial frame, $\mathbf{r}$, with coordinates measured in a non-inertial frame, $\mathbf{r}'$, by

$$\mathbf{r}(t) = \mathbf{r}'(t) + \mathbf{R}(t)$$

then the acceleration is given by

$$\ddot{\mathbf{r}}(t) = \ddot{\mathbf{r}}'(t) + \ddot{\mathbf{R}}(t).$$

Thus in the presence of a force $\mathbf{F}$ the equation of motion is

$$m\ddot{\mathbf{r}}(t) = m\ddot{\mathbf{r}}'(t) + m\ddot{\mathbf{R}}(t) = \mathbf{F}.$$

Viewed from the non-inertial frame one would write

$$m\ddot{\mathbf{r}}(t) = \mathbf{F}'$$

where the effective force $\mathbf{F}'$ is given by

$$\mathbf{F}' = \mathbf{F} - m\ddot{\mathbf{R}}(t)$$

a generalization of the result obtained in example 1.6.

So the fictitious force due to the non-inertial frame is given by $m\ddot{\mathbf{R}}$. The characteristic feature of a fictitious force is that it is proportional to mass, so that under a fictitious force the mass of the particle cancels from the equation of motion. It was the observation that the gravitational force also has this feature that led Einstein to regard gravitation as a fictitious force in the development of his general theory of relativity.

Example 5.2: Larmor's theorem

Consider a charged particle subject to a magnetic and an electric field. Show that the effect of the magnetic field can be eliminated (to first order) by transforming to a rotating frame of reference.

The force in an inertial frame is given by the Lorentz force

$$\mathbf{F} = m\,\frac{d^2\mathbf{r}}{dt^2} = Q\left\{\mathbf{E} + \frac{d\mathbf{r}}{dt} \times \mathbf{B}\right\}.$$

In a frame rotating with angular velocity $\boldsymbol{\omega}$ we have

$$\frac{d\mathbf{r}}{dt} = \dot{\mathbf{r}} + \boldsymbol{\omega} \times \mathbf{r}$$

and
$$\frac{d^2\mathbf{r}}{dt^2} = \ddot{\mathbf{r}} + 2\boldsymbol{\omega} \times \dot{\mathbf{r}} + \boldsymbol{\omega} \times (\boldsymbol{\omega} \times \mathbf{r}).$$

The equation of motion then becomes

$$m\ddot{\mathbf{r}} + 2m\boldsymbol{\omega} \times \dot{\mathbf{r}} + m\boldsymbol{\omega} \times (\boldsymbol{\omega} \times \mathbf{r})$$
$$= Q\mathbf{E} + Q\dot{\mathbf{r}} \times \mathbf{B} + Q(\boldsymbol{\omega} \times \mathbf{r}) \times \mathbf{B}.$$

Now the terms in $\dot{\mathbf{r}}$ will cancel if we equate

$$2m\boldsymbol{\omega} = -Q\mathbf{B}$$

that is, if we choose a reference frame rotating with angular velocity

$$\boldsymbol{\omega} = -\frac{Q}{2m}\mathbf{B}.$$

This gives the equation of motion

$$m\ddot{\mathbf{r}} = Q\mathbf{E} + \frac{Q^2}{2m}\mathbf{B} \times (\mathbf{B} \times \mathbf{r}).$$

For small magnetic fields the second term is second order in smallness and may be neglected. The effect of the magnetic field has thus been eliminated by going into a rotating frame. This result is known as Larmor's theorem.

Chapter 6
Lagrangian and Hamiltonian mechanics

6.1 Principle of least action

We now consider a completely different formulation of the laws of mechanics. Newton's second law, being expressed as a differential equation, relates the motion at a point to the motion close by. This may be regarded as a *local* view of the dynamics of the system. By contrast, we now adopt a *global* view—what can we say about the whole trajectory of our system? In other words, we shall (for the time being) concentrate our attention on the *solution* to the equations of motion rather than the equations themselves.

The actual trajectory of a dynamical system differs in a remarkable way from other trajectories taking the same time. There is a certain quantity which, if integrated with respect to time over the trajectory, gives a result which is a minimum for the actual path. All other trajectories give a greater value for the integral. For conservative systems the certain quantity is simply the difference between the kinetic energy and the potential energy! The integral is given the name *action*, so what we are talking about here is the Principle of Least Action, otherwise known as Hamilton's principle. The precise statement of the Principle of Least Action is as follows:

> The evolution of a dynamical system from time t_1 to time t_2 is such that the action $S(t_2, t_1)$ is a minimum with respect to arbitrary small changes in the trajectory.

The action is defined as the time integral of a function called the *Lagrangian, L*:

$$S = \int_{t_1}^{t_2} L \, dt$$

where for conservative systems

$$L = T - V$$

T being the kinetic energy and V the potential energy. For non-conservative systems L is more complex, as we shall see.

It is possible to derive the principle of least action from Newton's laws; this is tedious, but it was the historical route. Alternatively, one could require that something was minimized and then use arguments based on symmetry, Galilean invariance, etc., to find the form of the Lagrangian. However, we shall content ourselves with the middle road. Having postulated the form of the Lagrangian, we shall be happy when we find it leads to Newton's laws.

A particular advantage of this formulation is that one is dealing with quantities which are scalars — action and Lagrangian. They have the same value in any coordinate system, unlike the vectors of Newton's laws whose components depend on the coordinate system used. This feature of coordinate-independence means that any coordinate system may be used and one is free to choose coordinates suited to the problem.

Another advantage is that generalization to both quantum mechanics and relativity is facilitated by this formulation. In general relativity, particles move along 'geodesic' paths of least distance in a curved space–time. The various connections with quantum theory will be outlined in section 6.8.

6.2 Calculus of variations

The problem of finding a *function* that minimizes (or maximizes) the value of a quantity is known as the *calculus of variations*. We shall start by considering a problem with only one coordinate, which we denote by q. Our task then is to find the trajectory $q(t)$ for which the time integral of the Lagrangian is a minimum. At this stage we shall not specify how L depends on q. Our only restriction is that L depends only on q, its time derivative $\dot{q}$, and time t.

So we must minimize the action S, where

$$S = \int_{t_1}^{t_2} L\{q(t), \dot{q}(t), t\} \, \mathrm{d}t. \tag{6.1}$$

Let $q(t)$ be the actual trajectory and let us consider a slightly modified path

$$q(t) + \epsilon\phi(t) \tag{6.2}$$

where ϵ is a small quantity and $\phi(t)$ is *any* function of time subject to the restriction

$$\phi(t_1) = \phi(t_2) = 0 \tag{6.3}$$

since the end-points remain fixed (see Fig. 6.1).

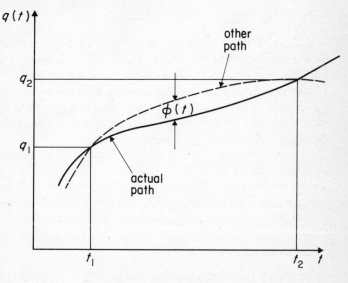

Fig. 6.1 Actual and varied trajectories between (ϕ_1, t_1) and (ϕ_2, t_2)

The condition that S be a minimum may be expressed by

$$\frac{\mathrm{d}S}{\mathrm{d}\epsilon} = 0$$

where now

$$S = \int_{t_1}^{t_2} L\{q + \epsilon\phi, \dot{q} + \epsilon\dot{\phi}, t\}\,\mathrm{d}t.$$

Upon differentiating with respect to ϵ

$$\frac{\mathrm{d}S}{\mathrm{d}\epsilon} = \int_{t_1}^{t_2} \left[\frac{\partial L}{\partial q}\phi + \frac{\partial L}{\partial \dot{q}}\dot{\phi}\right]\mathrm{d}t = 0.$$

Now the second term may be integrated by parts:

$$\int_{t_1}^{t_2} \frac{\partial L}{\partial \dot{q}}\frac{\mathrm{d}\phi}{\mathrm{d}t}\,\mathrm{d}t = \frac{\partial L}{\partial q}\phi(t)\Bigg|_{t_1}^{t_2} - \int_{t_1}^{t_2}\phi(t)\frac{\mathrm{d}}{\mathrm{d}t}\frac{\partial L}{\partial \dot{q}}\,\mathrm{d}t.$$

However, the first term is zero since there is no variation of the end-points (see equation [6.3]), so we are left with

$$\frac{\mathrm{d}S}{\mathrm{d}\epsilon} = \int_{t_1}^{t_2}\left[\frac{\partial L}{\partial q} - \frac{\mathrm{d}}{\mathrm{d}t}\frac{\partial L}{\partial \dot{q}}\right]\phi(t)\,\mathrm{d}t = 0.$$

This integral must be zero for arbitrary deviations $\phi(t)$, and this can only be possible if the square bracket is identically zero. We have thus obtained a differential equation for the Lagrangian that ensures that the action is minimized:

$$\frac{\partial L}{\partial q} - \frac{\mathrm{d}}{\mathrm{d}t}\frac{\partial L}{\partial \dot{q}} = 0. \qquad [6.4]$$

This is known as the *Euler-Lagrange equation*.

For several independent coordinates q_i ($i = 1, 2 \ldots n$) the generalization is simple. The action integral now has the form

$$S = \int_{t_1}^{t_2} L\{q_1 q_2 \ldots q_n, \dot{q}_1\dot{q}_2\ldots\dot{q}_n, t\}\,\mathrm{d}t$$

and S must be minimized with respect to changes in all of the q_i. This then leads to one Euler-Lagrange equation for each coordinate, i.e. a set of n Euler–Lagrange equations:

$$\frac{\partial L}{\partial q_i} - \frac{\mathrm{d}}{\mathrm{d}t}\frac{\partial L}{\partial \dot{q}_i} = 0. \qquad [6.5]$$

Recovery of Newton's laws

Let us start with the simplest problem, a particle of mass m moving in a straight line in a potential V. As a coordinate we shall use the distance along the line r. Thus for the kinetic and potential energies we have

$$T = \tfrac{1}{2}m\dot{r}^2 \qquad\qquad [6.6]$$
$$V = V(r). \qquad\qquad [6.7]$$

The Lagrangian is then

$$L(r,\dot{r}) = \tfrac{1}{2}m\dot{r}^2 - V(r) \qquad\qquad [6.8]$$

which may be substituted into the Euler-Lagrange equation for r:

$$\frac{\partial L}{\partial r} - \frac{d}{dt}\frac{\partial L}{\partial \dot{r}} = 0.$$

Evaluating the derivatives gives:

$$\frac{\partial L}{\partial r} = -\frac{\partial V}{\partial r}$$

$$\frac{\partial L}{\partial \dot{r}} = m\dot{r}$$

$$\frac{d}{dt}\frac{\partial L}{\partial \dot{r}} = m\ddot{r}.$$

The Euler-Lagrange equation then gives the result

$$m\ddot{r} = -\frac{\partial V}{\partial r} \qquad\qquad [6.9]$$

where, of course, we recognize Newton's second law, the force being given by the negative derivative of the potential energy (recall section 2.2).

The generalization to three dimensions in rectangular Cartesian coordinates is easy, since one obtains a similar equation for each coordinate:

$$m\ddot{r}_i = -\frac{\partial V}{\partial r_i}.$$

or

$$m\ddot{\mathbf{r}} = -\left\{\frac{\partial V}{\partial x}\mathbf{i} + \frac{\partial V}{\partial y}\mathbf{j} + \frac{\partial V}{\partial z}\mathbf{k}\right\}$$

and we have the gradient of V:

$$m\ddot{\mathbf{r}} = -\operatorname{grad} V. \tag{6.10}$$

Example 6.1

Obtain the equations of motion for a particle in a potential V in plane polar coordinates.

The polar coordinates r, ϕ are related to the Cartesian co-ordinates x, y by

$$\begin{aligned} x &= r\cos\phi \\ y &= r\sin\phi. \end{aligned} \tag{6.11}$$

The kinetic energy has already been obtained (exercise 5, chapter 2, Appendix 1):

$$T = \frac{m}{2}\{\dot{r}^2 + r^2\dot{\phi}^2\} \tag{6.12}$$

so that the Lagrangian is then

$$\begin{aligned} L &= T - V \\ &= \frac{m}{2}\{\dot{r}^2 + r^2\dot{\phi}^2\} - V(r, \phi). \end{aligned} \tag{6.13}$$

In this case we have two Euler–Lagrange equations for r and ϕ:

$$\frac{\partial L}{\partial r} - \frac{\mathrm{d}}{\mathrm{d}t}\frac{\partial L}{\partial \dot{r}} = 0$$

$$\frac{\partial L}{\partial \phi} - \frac{\mathrm{d}}{\mathrm{d}t}\frac{\partial L}{\partial \dot{\phi}} = 0.$$

Differentiating, we obtain

$$\frac{\partial L}{\partial r} = mr\dot{\phi}^2 - \frac{\partial V}{\partial r}$$

$$\frac{\partial L}{\partial \dot{r}} = m\dot{r}$$

$$\frac{\mathrm{d}}{\mathrm{d}t}\frac{\partial L}{\partial \dot{r}} = m\ddot{r}$$

$$\frac{\partial L}{\partial \phi} = -\frac{\partial V}{\partial \phi}$$

$$\frac{\partial L}{\partial \dot{\phi}} = mr^2\dot{\phi}.$$

One then obtains the equations

$$\left.\begin{array}{l} m\ddot{r} = mr\dot{\phi}^2 - \dfrac{\partial V}{\partial r} \\[2ex] \dfrac{\mathrm{d}}{\mathrm{d}t}(mr^2\dot{\phi}) = -\dfrac{\partial V}{\partial \phi}. \end{array}\right\} \qquad [6.14]$$

In the radial equation we have recovered the result of section 3.5, concerning the equivalent one-dimensional problem. We recognize the term $mr\dot{\phi}^2$ as the centrifugal force and the term $-\partial V/\partial r$ as the radial component of the applied force field.

The angular equation has been left as it is to show that the time derivative of the angular momentum, on the left-hand side, is equal to the tangential 'force' or torque on the right-hand side.

The previous example demonstrates the simplicity of the Lagrangian method. The equations of motion (in the form of the Euler-Lagrange equations) are the same whatever coordinates are used. That is why we adopted the new symbol q to represent the coordinates, as the coordinate system is now arbitrary. We then call q by the name *generalized coordinates*. It should be noted that the dimension of q need not be length; angles or even complicated variables may be used.

6.4   Symmetry and conservation laws

Complete information on the dynamical behaviour of a system is contained in the Lagrangian and the initial conditions. Now the Lagrangian may be expressed in terms of any coordinate system. In particular there may be a coordinate system in terms of which the Lagrangian is considerably simplified. Thus with a central force field, in Cartesian coordinates one will have both x and y (in a symmetrical combination) while in polar coordinates one has r but not ϕ in the Lagrangian. We see that a symmetry of the system, in this case rotational symmetry, reflects itself as a symmetry in the Lagrangian between x and y, and that another coordinate system may be found where the symmetry is made explicit by the vanishing of a coordinate.

Having chosen the natural coordinate system to reflect explicitly the symmetry in question through the absence of a coordinate, we shall see that the Euler-Lagrange equations will give us a conservation law. There are two cases to consider:

1. L independent of a coordinate q;
2. L independent of time t.

Considering the first case and the absence of a coordinate from L, one finds a generalized momentum conservation law. Denoting the missing coordinate by q_i, its Euler-Lagrange equation will be

$$\frac{\partial L}{\partial q_i} - \frac{\mathrm{d}}{\mathrm{d}t} \frac{\partial L}{\partial \dot{q}_i} = 0.$$

However since q_i is now absent from the Lagrangian, the first term $\partial L/\partial q_i$ is zero, so the equation becomes

$$\frac{\mathrm{d}}{\mathrm{d}t} \frac{\partial L}{\partial \dot{q}_i} = 0$$

or

$$\frac{\partial L}{\partial \dot{q}_i} = \text{constant}.$$

The absence of the coordinate q_i from the Lagrangian means that the quantity $\partial L/\partial \dot{q}_i$ is conserved. What is the physical significance of this conserved quantity? For Cartesian coordinates we have already evaluated this quantity

$$\frac{\partial L}{\partial \dot{x}} = m\dot{x}$$

the *momentum*. By analogy with this we define p_i, the *generalized momentum* or *canonical momentum* corresponding to (or conjugate to) the generalized coordinate q_i, by

$$p_i = \frac{\partial L}{\partial \dot{q}_i}.$$

Thus if a particular coordinate q_i does not appear in the expression for L then we infer that the corresponding generalized momentum is conserved.

Where the q_i is an angle we have conservation of angular momentum, but in more complex systems there may be no simple interpretation of the generalized momentum.

To summarize, if there is a symmetry in a dynamical system then we must:

1. recognize the symmetry (not always easy);
2. choose a coordinate system which naturally reflects the symmetry through the vanishing of a coordinate;
3. find the conjugate momentum, which is then a constant of the motion.

Turning now to the case where the Lagrangian is independent of time, we shall find that we are led to the law of energy conservation.

If L does not contain time explicitly, the only way it can change with time is through its dependence on the coordinates and the velocities. For simplicity, consider a system with only one coordinate. Then

$$\frac{\mathrm{d}L}{\mathrm{d}t} = \frac{\partial L}{\partial q} \frac{\mathrm{d}q}{\mathrm{d}t} + \frac{\partial L}{\partial \dot{q}} \frac{\mathrm{d}\dot{q}}{\mathrm{d}t}$$

since $\partial L / \partial t$ is zero in this case.

We use the expression for $\partial L / \partial q$ from the Euler–Lagrange equation

$$\frac{\partial L}{\partial q} = \frac{\mathrm{d}}{\mathrm{d}t} \frac{\partial L}{\partial \dot{q}}$$

so that

$$\frac{\mathrm{d}L}{\mathrm{d}t} = \left(\frac{\mathrm{d}}{\mathrm{d}t} \frac{\partial L}{\partial \dot{q}} \right) \dot{q} + \frac{\partial L}{\partial \dot{q}} \frac{\mathrm{d}\dot{q}}{\mathrm{d}t}.$$

However, this is the derivative of the product:

$$\frac{\mathrm{d}L}{\mathrm{d}t} = \frac{\mathrm{d}}{\mathrm{d}t}\left(\frac{\partial L}{\partial \dot{q}}\,\dot{q}\right)$$

and we may write this as

$$\frac{\mathrm{d}}{\mathrm{d}t}\left(\frac{\partial L}{\partial \dot{q}}\,\dot{q} - L\right) = 0$$

which may be integrated to give

$$\dot{q}\,\frac{\partial L}{\partial \dot{q}} - L = H, \text{a constant.}$$

The generalization to many coordinates therefore is simply

$$\sum_{i=1}^{n} \dot{q}_i\,\frac{\partial L}{\partial \dot{q}_i} - L = H, \text{a constant.}$$

The quantity H is a constant whenever the Lagrangian does not depend explicitly on time. When expressed as a function of the coordinates and momenta it is known as the *Hamiltonian* function.

For the special case of a conservative system the Hamiltonian has a particularly useful form. Since

$$L = T - V$$

the expression for the Hamiltonian is

$$H = \sum_{i=1}^{n} \dot{q}_i\,\frac{\partial L}{\partial \dot{q}_i} - T + V.$$

To evaluate the derivative $\partial L/\partial \dot{q}_i$ we assume that only the kinetic energy depends on the $\dot{q}_i$, and we also use the result that the kinetic energy always depends bilinearly on the generalized velocities (see exercise 2, chapter 6, Appendix 1):

$$T = \sum_{jk} M_{jk}\dot{q}_j\dot{q}_k.$$

Thus

$$\frac{\partial L}{\partial \dot{q}_i} = \frac{\partial T}{\partial \dot{q}_i} = \sum_j M_{ji}\dot{q}_j + \sum_k M_{ik}\dot{q}_k$$

but, since M_{jk} is symmetric this becomes

$$\frac{\partial L}{\partial \dot{q}_i} = 2\sum_j M_{ij}\dot{q}_j.$$

Multiplying by $\dot{q}_i$ and summing, we obtain

$$\sum_i \dot{q} \frac{\partial L}{\partial \dot{q}_i} = 2\sum_{ij} M_{ij}\dot{q}_i\dot{q}_j$$

but this is, of course, twice the kinetic energy:

$$\sum_i q_i \frac{\partial L}{\partial q_i} = 2T.$$

The Hamiltonian is then given by

$$H = 2T - T + V$$
$$= T + V$$

the total energy of the system!

To conclude, if the Lagrangian does not depend explicitly on time then the Hamiltonian is constant. Furthermore, if the potential energy does not depend on velocity then the Hamiltonian is numerically equal to the total energy.

6.5 Hamilton's equations

Hamilton took these arguments further. In the Lagrangian scheme one can transform to a new coordinate system at will, but once the n coordinates have been chosen, the other n variables in the equations, the velocities, are determined as the time derivative of the coordinates. Hamilton removed this subordinate feature of the second set of n variables by eliminating the velocities from the equations in favour of another set of variables, the generalized momenta.

One reason for this change is that the momenta are the very quantities to be conserved if any are, so that symmetries should be even more explicit in such a formulation. Another point is that whereas the Euler-Lagrange equations constitute n second-order equations, in the Hamiltonian method there are $2n$ first-order equations. However, perhaps the most important consideration is that whereas the function central to the Lagrangian scheme, the Lagrangian function, has no useful physical meaning (the difference between the kinetic and potential energies), the function that occurs in the Hamiltonian scheme is the Hamiltonian function, which, when conserved, is often the energy of the system—a very important quantity. So from one point of view, the Hamiltonian method may be seen to be intimately connected with symmetry and conservation.

To express the laws of mechanics in terms of the Hamiltonian let us evaluate its total differential.

Now

$$H = p\dot{q} - L(q, \dot{q}, t)$$

where we have explicitly written in the momentum p rather than the more cumbersome $\partial L/\partial \dot{q}$, and used only one coordinate for simplicity. Differentiating H gives

$$dH = p\,d\dot{q} + \dot{q}\,dp - \frac{\partial L}{\partial q}\,dq - \frac{\partial L}{\partial \dot{q}}\,d\dot{q} - \frac{\partial L}{\partial t}\,dt.$$

The first and fourth terms cancel, since $p = \partial L/\partial \dot{q}$, leaving

$$dH = \dot{q}\,dp - \frac{\partial L}{\partial q}\,dq - \frac{\partial L}{\partial t}\,dt$$

and since the Euler-Lagrange equation tells us that

$$\frac{\partial L}{\partial q} = \frac{d}{dt}\frac{\partial L}{\partial \dot{q}} = \frac{d}{dt}p = \dot{p}$$

we obtain

$$dH = \dot{q}\,dp - \dot{p}\,dq - \frac{\partial L}{\partial t}\,dt.$$

From this we obtain the equations for the partial derivatives of H:

$$\dot{q} = \frac{\partial H}{\partial p}, \qquad \dot{p} = -\frac{\partial H}{\partial q}, \qquad \frac{\partial H}{\partial t} = -\frac{\partial L}{\partial t}.$$

This is simply generalized to the case of n coordinates, giving Hamilton's equations:

$$\dot{q}_i = \frac{\partial H}{\partial p_i} \qquad \dot{p}_i = -\frac{\partial H}{\partial q_i}.$$

Evaluating the total time derivative of the Hamiltonian, we obtain

$$\frac{\mathrm{d}H}{\mathrm{d}t} = \dot{q}\,\frac{\mathrm{d}p}{\mathrm{d}t} - \dot{p}\,\frac{\mathrm{d}q}{\mathrm{d}t} - \frac{\partial L}{\partial t}\ .$$

The first two terms cancel by virtue of Hamilton's equations and the last term is $\partial H/\partial t$, so that one has

$$\frac{\mathrm{d}H}{\mathrm{d}t} = \frac{\partial H}{\partial t}\ .$$

Thus if H does not depend explicitly on time then it is constant.

Recall that the Lagrange equations are independent of the choice of coordinate system. A transformation from one set of coordinates to another is known as a *point transformation*. The Lagrange equations are therefore invariant under point transformations, but one has no choice in the other half of the variables used, the velocities.

However, when using Hamilton's equations the choice of variables is greater, and one has a certain freedom also in the choice of the momenta. Those transformations of coordinates and momenta that leave Hamilton's equations unchanged are known as *canonical transformations*.

Finally we might note that, having embarked on our journey from Newton's laws, passed the principle of last action and Lagrange's equations, and having arrived at Hamilton's equations, we have gone full circle. Newton's second law in component form is

$$m\ddot{r_i} = F_i$$

or, in terms of momentum and a potential energy function,

$$\dot{p_i} = -\frac{\partial V}{\partial r_i}\ .$$

But this bears a striking similarity to the Hamiltonian equation

$$\dot{p_i} = -\frac{\partial H}{\partial q_i}$$

when we realize that in Cartesian coordinates the kinetic energy is independent of the coordinates, so that

$$\frac{\partial V}{\partial r_i} = \frac{\partial H}{\partial r_i}.$$

In other words we are back at what are essentially Newton's equations, but with a much greater generality.

6.6 Charged particle in an electromagnetic field

We have seen that the magnetic force is awkward in that it cannot be expressed as the gradient of a scalar potential energy function. So if the magnetic force could be treated from the Lagrangian point of view, the Lagrangian function is certainly not the simple $T - V$. How, then, should we proceed? In the spirit of our philosophy, as outlined in section 6.1, all we ask for is a Lagrangian that gives the correct equations of motion.

We shall see that the following Lagrangian does just that:

$$L = \tfrac{1}{2}m\dot{r}^2 - Q\phi(\mathbf{r}, t) + Q\dot{\mathbf{r}} \cdot \mathbf{A}(\mathbf{r}, t)$$

where Q is the charge and ϕ and $\mathbf{A}$ are the scalar and vector potentials in terms of which the electric and magnetic fields are given by

$$\mathbf{B} = \text{curl } \mathbf{A}$$
$$\mathbf{E} = -\text{grad } \phi - \partial \mathbf{A}/\partial t.$$

The second term in the Lagrangian is the potential energy. The third term is a new one and it takes account of the magnetic field through its dependence on the vector potential $\mathbf{A}$.

In terms of the coordinates r_i, where $r_1 = x$, $r_2 = y$, $r_3 = z$, we can evaluate the derivatives necessary for the Euler–Lagrange equations:

$$\frac{\partial L}{\partial r_i} = -Q \frac{\partial \phi}{\partial r_i} + Q \sum_j \dot{r}_j \frac{\partial A_j}{\partial r_i}$$

$$\frac{\partial L}{\partial \dot{r}_i} = m\dot{r}_i + QA_i.$$

This second equation must be differentiated with respect to time:

$$\frac{\mathrm{d}}{\mathrm{d}t} \frac{\partial L}{\partial \dot{r}_i} = m\ddot{r}_i + Q \frac{\mathrm{d}A_i}{\mathrm{d}t}$$

$$= m\ddot{r}_i + Q\frac{\partial A_i}{\partial t} + Q\sum_j \frac{\partial A_i}{\partial r_j}\dot{r}_j.$$

Thus the Euler-Lagrange equation

$$\frac{\partial L}{\partial r_i} - \frac{d}{dt}\frac{\partial L}{\partial \dot{r}_i} = 0$$

gives

$$-Q\frac{\partial\phi}{\partial r_i} + Q\sum_j\dot{r}_j\frac{\partial A_j}{\partial r_i} - m\ddot{r}_i - Q\frac{\partial A_i}{\partial t} - Q\sum_j\frac{\partial A_i}{\partial r_j}\dot{r}_j = 0$$

or

$$m\ddot{r}_i = -Q\left(\frac{\partial\phi}{\partial r_i} + \frac{\partial A_i}{\partial t}\right) + Q\sum_j\dot{r}_j\left(\frac{\partial A_j}{\partial r_i} - \frac{\partial A_i}{\partial r_j}\right).$$

The first bracket we see contains the expression for the ith component of the electric field. The last bracket contains the k component of curl $\mathbf{A}$, or $\mathbf{B}$, the magnetic field. Permuting the indices for the three values of j in the sum, the second term then becomes the ith component of $\dot{\mathbf{r}} \times \mathbf{B}$. We have then recovered the equation for motion under the Lorentz force:

$$m\ddot{\mathbf{r}} = Q\{\mathbf{E} + \dot{\mathbf{r}} \times \mathbf{B}\}$$

and we have thus justified the expression for the Lagrangian.

On the way we evaluated the conjugate momentum:

$$p_i = \frac{\partial L}{\partial \dot{r}_i} = m\dot{r}_i + QA_i$$

or, in vector form,

$$\mathbf{p} = m\dot{\mathbf{r}} + Q\mathbf{A}.$$

It is different from the common mechanical momentum $m\dot{\mathbf{r}}$, but in the present form it reflects the symmetry of the system. In particular it is the quantity $m\dot{\mathbf{r}} + Q\mathbf{A}$ that is conserved in the presence of a magnetic field if the coordinates do not appear in the Lagrangian (no electric field). Furthermore, in the presence of a magnetic field it is this conjugate momentum that goes over to quantum mechanics as the momentum operator.

Finally, let us evaluate the Hamiltonian for the system to see if it corresponds with the energy, even with such a peculiar momentum:

$$H = \sum_i p_i \dot{r}_i - L$$

$$= \tfrac{1}{2}m[\mathbf{p} - Q\mathbf{A}]^2 + q\phi.$$

Since $\mathbf{p}$ includes the term in $Q\mathbf{A}$ we see that we do obtain the energy $T + V$.

6.7 Poisson brackets

In this section we briefly examine what are known as Poisson brackets. These were originally introduced into the framework of mechanics in the study of planetary perturbations. Today their importance is in their relation to the commutators of quantum mechanics, and this will be discussed in the next section. Here we shall content ourselves with the definition of Poisson brackets, together with a discussion of a few of their relevant properties.

Given a dynamical system with a set of coordinates q_i and a set of conjugate momenta p_i, the Poisson bracket of two dynamical variables $U(p_i, q_i)$ $V(p_i, q_.)$ is written

$$\{U, V\}.$$

It is defined by

$$\{U, V\} = \sum_i \frac{\partial U}{\partial q_i} \frac{\partial V}{\partial p_i} - \frac{\partial U}{\partial p_i} \frac{\partial V}{\partial q_i}.$$

We summarize some properties that follow from this definition.

1. Anti-symmetry:

$$\{U, V\} = -\{V, U\}$$

from which follows

$$\{U, U\} = 0.$$

2. Linearity, for constant a, b:

$$\{aU + bV, W\} = a\{U, W\} + b\{V, W\}.$$

3. Jacobi's identity:

$$\{U, \{V, W\}\} + \{V, \{W, U\}\} + \{W, \{U, V\}\} = 0.$$

Hamilton's equations may be expressed simply in terms of

Poisson brackets. Let us put V equal to the Hamiltonian in the definition. Then:

$$\{U, H\} = \sum_i \frac{\partial U}{\partial q_i} \frac{\partial H}{\partial p_i} - \frac{\partial U}{\partial p_i} \frac{\partial H}{\partial q_i}.$$

However from Hamilton's equations

$$\frac{\partial H}{\partial p_i} = \dot{q}_i, \qquad -\frac{\partial H}{\partial q_i} = \dot{p}_i$$

so that

$$\{U, H\} = \sum_i \frac{\partial U}{\partial q_i} \dot{q}_i + \frac{\partial U}{\partial p_i} \dot{p}_i$$

i.e. the implicit rate of change of U due to its dependence on the dynamical variables q_i, p_i. The total rate of change of U may then be written:

$$\frac{dU}{dt} = \{U, H\} + \frac{\partial U}{\partial t}. \tag{6.15}$$

This is the equation of motion for the variable U in Poisson bracket form.

An important Poisson bracket is that between a coordinate and its conjugate momentum:

$$\{q_j, p_k\} = \sum_i \frac{\partial q_j}{\partial q_i} \frac{\partial p_k}{\partial p_i} - \frac{\partial q_j}{\partial p_i} \frac{\partial p_k}{\partial q_i}.$$

The second term vanishes and we are left with the first term. Now $\partial q_j / \partial q_i$ is zero unless $i = j$, in which case it is equal to unity. A similar argument holds for $\partial p_k / \partial p_i$, so that we obtain the result

$$\{q_j, p_k\} = 1 \qquad j = k$$
$$= 0 \qquad j \neq k.$$

6.8 Connections with quantum mechanics

There have been various formulations of quantum mechanics, two dating back to the early days. Schrödinger developed a differential equation while Heisenberg worked with matrices. Later the two systems were unified and other formulations were devised. We shall not adopt a historical perspective in this section; rather we shall follow the course of this chapter and point out the various connections with quantum mechanics along the way.

We start with the principle of least action itself. In quantum mechanics we cannot speak of the trajectory of a system. Various trajectories are possible and all we can say is that if we start from A then there is a certain probability that we shall get to B. However, we cannot even add the probabilities for the various trajectories, since there can be interference between the different paths. Instead we talk of the *probability amplitude* for each trajectory. These (complex) quantities are added for each path and the magnitude of the square gives the probability that we have gone from A to B somehow.

Classically only one path is important, the actual path for which the action is least. Quantum mechanically, other paths must be considered, and they can be considered from the point of view of the action. This line of reasoning was suggested by Dirac and followed by Feynman. He postulated that the probability amplitude associated with a particular trajectory was related to the action S by the expression $\exp(iS/\hbar)$ where $\hbar$ is Planck's constant. The quantum mechanical amplitude is then obtained by summing over all paths and the result found to be in agreement with other formulations. In the classical limit where S is very much larger than $\hbar$ only the extreme value of S contributes as, away from the minimum, the exponentials oscillate so rapidly that the amplitudes of all other paths interfere destructively and cancel out. Thus the classical path dominates.

Another approach to quantum mechanics, based on the ideas of Heisenberg but formalized by Dirac, relies on the fact that in quantum mechanics observable quantities are represented by operators (such as matrices). An important property of matrices and operators in general is that they do not commute, i.e. the order in which you multiply them matters. On discovering this Heisenberg almost gave up the work, but it turns out that this non-commutativity is vital to the theory. The commutator of two operators $\hat{u}$, $\hat{v}$, representing the observables u and v, is defined as

$$[\hat{u}, \hat{v}] = \hat{u}\hat{v} - \hat{v}\hat{u}.$$

Based on the definition above we see that the commutator of two operators obeys the same algebra as the Poisson brackets, properties *a, b* and *c*. Dirac was inspired to conjecture that the commutator was the quantum mechanical Poisson bracket. He made the identification

$$\{u, v\} \sim i\hbar \, [\hat{u}, \hat{v}]$$

where the i is necessary to ensure that observed quantities are real and the $\hbar$ keeps things dimensionally correct.

One then has the remarkable result that, once the classical equations of a system are written in terms of the Poisson brackets, the quantum equation may be written down directly.

From equation [6.15] we can immediately write down the quantum equation for the operator $\hat{U}$:

$$\frac{d\hat{U}}{dt} = i\hbar \, [\hat{H}, \hat{U}] + \frac{\partial \hat{U}}{\partial t}.$$

This is called the *Heisenberg equation*.

Transformation from one set of variables to another is effected in this scheme through what we call unitary transformations and these turn out to be the analogue of the canonical transformation of Hamiltonian mechanics mentioned in section 6.5.

There is a further formulation due to Schwinger, using a Lagrangian operator, but this has not proved too popular.

Last, but not least, is the formulation of Schrödinger in terms of a differential equation. This may be related to a differential equation obeyed by the action function, but that analogy is not too helpful at the elementary level. This is unfortunate since the Schrödinger method is certainly the most popular introductory way to regard quantum mechanics.

Appendix 1
Exercises

Chapter 2

1   What are the features of the forces given in example 2.2? Describe a situation where each one may be found.

2   A very light particle of mass m and velocity v collides head-on with a stationary particle of large mass M. Show that on colliding the velocity of the moving particle is approximately reversed, while the massive particle gains a velocity $V \sim 2vm/M$.

3   Demonstrate that a central force is always conservative by showing that it can be obtained from a potential energy function which depends only on the distance from the force centre.

4   The potential energy of interaction between a proton and a neutron may be approximated by an expression of the form

$$V(r) = \frac{c}{r} \exp(-r/a)$$

where r is the separation and a and c are constants. (This also approximates to the interaction between two electrons in the electron 'sea' of a metal.) What force does this potential energy represent?

5   Show that for motion in a plane the kinetic energy of a body of mass m is given in polar coordinates r, ϕ by
$$T = \tfrac{1}{2}m(\dot{r}^2 + r^2\dot{\phi}^2).$$

Chapter 3

1   A popular baby's toy is a doll (or other object) attached to a long spring. Regarding this as an elastic pendulum, explain the motion

of the system in terms of the conservation laws.

2 A rifle bullet weighing 10 g hits a suspended 1 kg block of wood. If the impact causes the block to rise 3 cm, what was the velocity of the bullet?

3 The Lennard–Jones potential between two atoms may be represented by

$$V(r) = -\frac{A}{r^6} + \frac{B}{r^{12}}.$$

Sketch the form of this interaction and describe the features of the atomic motion.

4 Obtain equation [3.31] for the length of the Runge–Lenz vector by substituting the expression for a conic (equation [3.29]) with the orbit equation (equation [3.20]).

5 Estimate the errors in Kepler's third law for the outer planets of the solar system.

6 Calculate the period of oscillation for a particle moving in a power-law potential $V(x) = ax^n$ for even integral n (hard).

Chapter 4

1 Scattering under an inverse-square-law force may be treated in terms of the Runge–Lenz vector. Show that the vector is given by

$$A = \mu(2Es e_0 \times n - k e_0)$$

where E and s are the energy and impact parameter of the incident particle, e_0 is the unit vector in the initial direction of the projectile and n is the unit vector normal to both e_0 and the position of the particle with respect to the force centre. In what direction does this vector point, in terms of the particle motion? Hence obtain equation [4.26] for the scattering angle.

2 Two solid spheres of identical material have diameters d_1 and d_2. What is the ratio of their terminal velocities?

3 Obtain an expression for the period of rotation of a binary star of two equal masses.

4 A hyperbola has two branches. Show that in scattering from a $1/r$ potential one branch corresponds to an attractive interaction while the other corresponds to a repulsive interaction.

5 A fireman aims his hose directly at a wall. Demonstrate that

the interaction between the fireman and the wall obeys Newton's third law.

Chapter 5

1 Calculate the effect the rotation of the earth has on the value of g measured: (a) at the equator; (b) at the pole.
2 Consider the general rigid-body motion of a cube, a sphere and a right cylinder. For which two of these is the motion similar, and why?
3 Show that a triangular plate has the same moment of inertia as a system of three point masses at the mid-point of the triangle. What is the mass of the point masses in terms of the mass of the plate?
4 Show that a satellite a distance r away from the centre of the earth and rotating around the earth with angular frequency ω is accelerating towards the earth with an acceleration $r\omega^2$. Calculate the radius of the orbit for which the satellite appears to be stationary to an earthbound observer.
5 Derive equation [5.2] relating the velocity in a fixed and rotating frame algebraically using the chain rule for differentiation.
6 Why are rockets constructed as a number of stages rather than a single object?

Chapter 6

1 Show that the momentum conjugate to an angle is the ordinary angular momentum (in the absence of a velocity-dependent force).
2 In terms of the generalized velocities $\dot{q}_i$, show that the kinetic energy of a dynamical system may be written as

$$T = \sum_{ij} M_{ij} \dot{q}_i \dot{q}_j.$$

Obtain an expression for the matrix elements M_{ij}. Hint: the generalized coordinates q_i and a set of Cartesian coordinates are related through a set of equations:

$$x_1 = x_1(q_1 \, q_2 \ldots q_n)$$
$$x_2 = x_2(q_1 \, q_2 \ldots q_n)$$
$$\vdots \qquad \vdots \quad \vdots \quad \vdots \quad \vdots \vdots \vdots \vdots$$
$$x_n = x_n(q_1 \, q_2 \ldots q_n).$$

3   Use Hamilton's equations and the expression for H in the presence of a magnetic field to obtain the equation of motion for a charged particle in a magnetic field.

4   Show that the Poisson bracket between any two Cartesian coordinates is zero. Show that the Poisson bracket of the angular-momentum components L_x, L_y, L_z is given by

$$\{L_x, L_y\} = L_z$$

and cyclic permutations thereof.

5   Show that in cylindrical polar coordinates ρ, θ, z, the Lagrangian of a particle of mass m and charge Q may be written as

$$L = \tfrac{1}{2}m(\dot{\rho}^2 + \rho^2\dot{\theta}^2 + \dot{z}^2) + Q(\dot{\rho}A_\rho + \rho\dot{\theta}A_\theta + \dot{z}A_z) - Q\phi$$

where $\mathbf{A}$ and ϕ are the vector and scalar potentials respectively. Show that the canonical angular momentum p_θ differs from the common angular momentum by an amount $\tfrac{1}{2}BQ\rho^2$ where B is a constant magnetic field in the z direction, related to the vector potential by

$$A_\theta = \tfrac{1}{2}B\rho.$$

Demonstrate that this extra angular momentum is precisely that gained when the particle enters such a magnetic field.

Appendix 2
Answers to exercises

Chapter 2

4 $F(\mathbf{r}) = \dfrac{c}{r}\left(\dfrac{1}{r} + \dfrac{1}{a}\right) \exp\left(-r/a\right)\, \hat{\mathbf{r}}$

Chapter 3

2 77 m s^{-1}

6 $\dfrac{2}{n}\left(\dfrac{4E}{a}\right)^{1/n}\dfrac{M}{2E}\ \Gamma^{2}\!\left(\dfrac{1}{n}\right)\!\Big/\Gamma\!\left(\dfrac{2}{n}\right)$

(This is a very difficult question. $\Gamma(x)$ is the gamma function, essentially a generalization of the factorial function for non-integral arguments.)

Chapter 4

2 $v_1/v_2 = d_1/d_2$

3 $\sqrt{2\pi^3/G}$

Chapter 5

1 Reduction of 0.34% at equator. No effect at the pole.

3 Each mass is one-third of the mass of the plate.

4 $4.24 \times 10^7 \text{ m}$.

Index

Series Editor:
Professor R. J. Blin-Stoyle, FRS
Professor of Theoretical Physics, University of Sussex

The aim of the *Student Physics Series* is to cover the material
required for a first degree course in physics in a series of concise,
clear and readable texts. Each volume will cover one of the usual
sections of the physics degree course and will concentrate on
covering the essential features of the subject. The texts will thus
provide a core course in physics that all students should be
expected to acquire, and to which more advanced work can be
related according to ability. By concentrating on the essentials,
the texts should also allow a valuable perspective and
accessibility not normally attainable through the more usual
textbooks.

RELATIVITY PHYSICS

Relativity Physics covers all the material required for a first
course in relativity. Beginning with an examination of the paradoxes
that arose in applying the principle of relativity to the two great
pillars of nineteenth-century physics—classical mechanics and
electromagnetism—Dr Turner shows how Einstein resolved these
problems in a spectacular and brilliantly intuitive way. The implications
of Einstein's postulates are then discussed and the book concludes
with a discussion of the charged particle in the electromagnetic field.

The text incorporates details of the most recent experiments and
includes applications to high-energy physics, astronomy, and solid state
physics. Exercises with answers are included for the student.

R. E. Turner

Dr Roy Turner is Reader in Theoretical Physics at the University of
Sussex.

ISBN 0-7102-0001-3
About 128 pp., 198 mm x 129 mm, diagrams, April 1984

ELECTRICITY AND MAGNETISM

Electromagnetism is basic to our understanding of the properties of
matter and yet is often regarded a difficult part of a first degree course.
In this book Professor Dobbs provides a concise and elegant account of
the subject, covering all the material required by a student taking such
a course. Although concentrating on the essentials of the subject,
interesting applications are discussed in the text. Vector operators
are introduced at the appropriate points and exercises, with answers,
are included for the student.

E. R. Dobbs

Professor Roland Dobbs is Hildred Carlile Professor of Physics at
the University of London.

ISBN 0-7102-0157-5
About 128 pp., 198 mm x 129 mm, diagrams, April 1984